Resilient Communities

How Parents and Educators Transform the World Despite the Impact of Trauma and Stress

Leanne Porter M.Ed.

Please visit: LeanneLPorter.com

Copyright 2018 Leanne Porter
All rights reserved. No part of this book may be reproduced in any manner without written permission from the author.

Table of Contents

PART I

Introduction

Terms

Chapter one   Overview of Trauma and Attachment

PART II

Terms

Chapter two   Behavior and Discipline at School

Chapter three   Behavior and Discipline at Home

Chapter four   Educators Building Resiliency

Chapter five   Parents Promoting Resiliency

Chapter six   Characteristics of Your Own Resiliency

Chapter seven   Advocating for Your Child at School

Chapter eight   Educators Partnering with Parents

PART III

Conclusion

Acknowledgements

Appendix of Activities

Introduction

This book offers a comprehensive approach for parents and educators to make every day better for children.

Fourteen years ago, I became interested in post-adoption work. I worked with an amazing group of women who supported children who were adopted from state custody. We became passionate about the lives of these children and we wanted to help them heal from their troubling pasts. Our job was to figure out the roadblocks that parents met, especially when it came to severe behavior challenges.

We soaked up all of the information that we could about Reactive Attachment Disorder to the point where we became experts on the topic. We started teaching parents and educators about attachment and the impact of a traumatic past. We created trainings that became very popular in schools throughout Vermont. The more I provided the training the more stories I heard about the impact of trauma on school systems. I learned that what is most challenging for educators and for parents is difficult behavior. Attachment challenges, trauma, and extreme stress are the causes of most of the behavior issues we have in schools. How we treat difficult behavior can be more universal than I once suspected.

After leaving my work with the State of Vermont I spent one year as an Assistant Principal in an elementary and middle school. I wanted an opportunity to see first-hand how teachers deal with the behaviors caused by stress today and what they understand about the impact of trauma. I wanted to try out many of my strategies and techniques in a school environment. The school was in a small rural town where intergenerational trauma was taking over the community. I learned more than I could have imagined from the staff and students. I am now able to offer many practical interventions that were tested out by fabulous teachers in the harshest of situations.

There are many students today who have dealt with unimaginable situations. Then there are students who live and learn next to these very troubled students. We have overworked teachers who are suffering from vicarious trauma trying to teach all students to live and work in our constantly changing society.

<u>I want to clearly state what a "trauma-informed" school is not.</u>

Becoming a trauma-informed school does not mean that teachers help troubled students become less disruptive. It shouldn't be about how children who have experienced trauma impact the rest of the system.

It is about the system itself.

The number of people who have experienced trauma is growing. There is a continuum where the survivors of trauma can be placed. The continuum ranges from people who have experienced an upbringing filled with tension but with some stability, to people who have lived through horrific prolonged abuse and neglect.

There are also folks living and learning in the same systems who have not had long-term or damaging exposure to trauma. These people are still impacted by trauma on a daily basis.

In this book, we have considered trauma as a piece of the dysfunctional system and not the dysfunction. This book is for all educators and parents who want to have a positive impact on the children in their lives and the community as a whole.

<u>What is a Trauma-Informed system?</u>

A trauma-informed system understands the developmental and long-term effects of trauma on a person. Everyone in the system knows the signs and symptoms of trauma. They understand and empathize with the impact this has on the child's ability to learn within the school setting.

What is a Resilient Community?

A community that is resilient knows all of the above but also understands it's limitations. They won't be stuck by limitations but they will work together to overcome them.

A resilient community will find resources that can be added to the system to help the community flourish. They recognize when they need to go outside of their school community for an even greater level of support.

The most important thing that a resilient community understands is what their capacity is for handling trauma and how to strengthen and build that capacity.

TERMS

Stress, many people do not think about stress as a physical response in one's body. It begins with a difficult situation but stress is your body's reaction to the stressor. Stress is your body's way of responding to any kind of demand or threat. When we want to reduce stress we have to start with our bodies. We can't always remove the stressor but learning how we each handle stress is the key to becoming more resilient. There are different levels of stress:

> ***Adaptable Stress:*** Is a normal part of life. It is short term and is not damaging like the other types of stress because it helps us to grow. Changing jobs is an example of adaptable stress.

> ***Tolerable Stress:*** Is harder to overcome. It is a process but with a strong foundation and support we can get through it. Death of a pet is an example of tolerable stress.

> ***Toxic Stress:*** Is prolonged chronic stress. It has a physical and emotional impact on the person that is lasting. Domestic violence falls within this type of stress.

Anxiety, or extreme apprehension and worry, is a normal reaction to stressful situations. Learning how our body responds while our anxiety level is rising is key to improving our overall state of well-being. It is also key for improving social skills.

Shame is the basis for most negative behavior. It is a derivative of anxiety.

Resiliency seems to be a new term being used in schools today. It is a good term because in the past our trauma studies have shown the hopeless side of trauma's impact. Teaching students how to be resilient is the answer to "what can we do about the problem?" The way each of us responds after a letdown is important. Having this information for ourselves and about our students can have a giant impact on our lives. It is imperative that we believe that we can improve our capacity for resilience and to make an effort to do so.

When we break resiliency down into the responses and behaviors that make up our choices and our ability to learn, we are talking about **self-regulation**. Self-regulation is learned; we are not born with it. It is how we cope with stress. Self-regulation is how we manage our behavior in accordance with the stimulus. This takes a certain amount of **mindfulness** – another term we are hearing about in education circles. Mindfulness has to do with paying attention to what you are thinking and feeling, more information in part II.

All of these concepts are tightly interwoven to make up our ability to do well. In this book we will delve into more detail about each of them. We will offer many tools to teach and practice resiliency, self-regulation, and mindfulness. These tools will help us to cope with trauma histories, stress, and anxiety for ourselves and for the children in our lives.

Questions to consider while reading this book:

What is trauma?

What is resilience?

Why are educators so passionate about the impact of trauma?

Do parents understand what it means for their school to be trauma-informed?

Do parents understand how trauma relates to themselves, their family, and their community?

How do teachers define a trauma-informed school? How does that look in the classroom?

Chapter 1
Overview of Trauma and Attachment

This chapter contains as many questions as it has answers. It is meant to be a process that you can go through to deeply understand the impact of attachment. As I stated in the introduction, I provided a workshop for schools in Vermont for over 10 years. The workshop started out with a group of us teaching about the effects of reactive attachment related issues. It morphed into a developmental trauma workshop. We provided this workshop to many schools, conferences, and to groups of parents. Over the years, and as I stopped working with my talented colleagues, my own version of a trauma workshop emerged. It then turned into a trauma and resilience workshop.

It was an interactive program that was always well received. I am going to begin this book by offering you this workshop in written form. It is going to be interactive; you will be asked to think about a lot of things and answer many questions. At the end of the chapter, you will find a reference of answers that workshop participants and colleagues gave to the questions in the chapter. I don't want to give them away too soon because I want you to think about them from your own perspective. Use the lines provided to brainstorm. Write down what comes immediately to mind. You can go back and add more notes once you complete the chapter.

Two of the most influential women who started the attachment workshops were Karen Crowley and Nancy Birge. We provided them in conjunction with Casey Family Services, Easter Seals Vermont, and The Vermont Adoption Consortium. Thank you, Karen and Nancy.

If possible, start this experience by watching the video clip:

Still Face Experiment: Dr. Edward Tronick
(See resource page for the link)

Developmentally we know that the first three years of life has a very impressive impact on the brain. But how?

1 - During the first year of life what can a baby learn?
_____
_____
_____
_____
_____

2 - How does that baby learn?

_____
_____
_____
_____
_____

It helps to break it down developmentally. Also, consider how an infant's brain is developing at a rapid pace during this stage.

How the baby learns is the crucial piece of the attachment puzzle. It also helps us to understand how attachment and trauma are related.

If a baby who is three months old is placed in a white room snuggled comfortably in a car seat, what will she be learning?

Most likely not much, because if she is comfortable she will probably tune out and go to sleep.

If we place that same baby in her mother's arms, **now what can she learn?**

- the physical stimulation of warm touch
- language through the mother's sounds
- social skills through the mother's eye contact

What else can she learn?

Cognitive development, physical development, social-emotional development, and language development are all impacted. Try to imagine these areas of development and what her presence may teach the baby.

_____
_____
_____
_____
_____

Now let's skip ahead to when the baby turns two.

What developmental changes impact learning?

- the child becomes mobile
- the child begins to use language (usually learns to tell you "no")

What other changes can you think of?

_____
_____
_____
_____
_____

I don't think we should even imagine leaving a two-year-old alone in a white room; that probably would not go well. But what does the mother, father, or other caretaker do to aid in this child's learning?

- teaches them what is safe and not safe so they can learn from self-exploration.
- language from communication

What else do they learn from caretakers at this stage?

_____
_____
_____
_____
_____

All of this learning is very important but there is even more to it than that.

There is a rhythm and a cycle to the give and take relationship between a caretaker and a child. This cycle teaches the child the fundamentals of what they will need in life.

This is how the attachment cycle works:

 A baby feels uncomfortable because they are wet, hungry, tired, or stressed in countless possible ways.

 The baby cries.

The caregiver soothes the baby and takes care of his need.

This happens over and over during that first year of life.

This teaches the infant a great deal. It teaches them that they can trust the adults in their world. It also teaches them cause and effect thinking. Every time they cry the person shows up. This very personal back and forth is the foundation of communication.

What else could this interaction teach the baby?

_____
_____
_____
_____
_____

They learn that it is okay to make mistakes. They understand that it is a part of testing out the world. There is a basic understanding that there is someone protecting them if they mess up too badly.

Not only does the baby learn from his interactions with his caregiver, but the caregiver gets a lot back from the interaction. It is a nice warm feeling when your baby is soothed, and you feel connected.

In a speech I heard years ago the presenter said that there is a soft place in your neck that a baby instinctually sticks her head into, that releases a hormone that makes you feel attached. I think the baby's soft hair and baby smell helps too.

Now comes the sad question.

What does the baby learn when the caregiver is not present? What happens if the caregiver has an angry or unpredictable response to the child's discomfort? What if the child experiences pain as a result of her arousal?

What does a child in this situation learn about the world?

- not to trust
- the world is unpredictable
- that she is unimportant and doesn't matter to anyone

What else do they learn about their environment, thus the world?

_____
_____
_____
_____
_____

How does it impact the child's developmental learning that we described above?

_____
_____
_____
_____
_____

Imagine a child in both of these scenarios. One child has a healthy attachment cycle and the other one does not. Say the second child experienced neglect on and off during the first three years of his life. Both children show up to school. How might their behaviors, traits, or attitudes look to the new kindergarten teacher?

For example, a securely attached child might be able to handle transitions better. He might be able to socialize with other children right away. He might have an age-appropriate attention span.

A child who has had a difficult or a "traumatic" start to life might come to kindergarten with a very different set of behaviors, traits, or attitudes. He might be extremely shy or overly aggressive. He may have a hard time paying attention. He probably won't trust adults right away which could impact his attitude.

What other characteristics or behaviors might we see in a child with an unhealthy early attachment cycle?

Use your knowledge of what a neglected child learns about their environment to answer this question.

_____
_____
_____
_____
_____

How might the interruption of the caregiver and child relationship cycle impact a person?

_____
_____
_____
_____
_____

There are many things that can cause a disruption to the attachment cycle. Some are minor and some are devastating. The timing of the traumatic events and the duration of them are two factors that impact the person's development. Another very important factor is if the child has another caregiver or other people in their lives that add some balance. Also, if the child had a strong attachment before a traumatic event, they may be better off than a child who never had a solid attachment.

Some possible causes of attachment disruption might be:

- neglect
- physical abuse
- witnessing domestic violence
- homelessness
- substance abuse
- any type of pervasive stress on a parent such as poverty, the death of a family member, hospitalization, etc.

I am sure you can think of many more examples:

_____
_____
_____
_____
_____

TRAUMA VISUALIZATION

I want to switch gears now and give you a visualization exercise that demonstrates some important points about trauma.

Imagine that you are walking in the woods with a coworker (a mentor) whom you admire. You are walking down a path and she is sharing information that you find interesting. You are a bit distracted and the path becomes more narrow as you walk. Suddenly, you notice that you have approached a large bear with her cub.

I am assuming that this would be a frightening experience for you; we know how mama bears protect their cubs.

What is happening in your body? I am not asking what you might do, but how your body is reacting. You may start to turn red, sweat, breathe heavy, clench your fists (and other body parts). Your heart is probably racing. Think of all of the ways that adrenalin affects you physically:

_____
_____
_____
_____
_____

Now think about what you would do.

There are three possible reactions to extreme unpredictable stress: fight, flight, or freeze. This happens before you think.

You either try to run away, you try to fight your way out of it or you become incapacitated and are very still. These responses are our brain's way of protecting us from danger. Our mind becomes temporarily dormant and our bodies take over.

A few years ago, when I was giving a school workshop, there was an announcement over the intercom that there was a student with a gun on campus. The teachers and guidance counselors snapped into action, they closed the door, locked the windows etc. The parent in the room sat dazed. Guess what I did. I started to run. Only about two steps before I realized that there was no place to go. It was silly, really, but my body acted before my mind was engaged. All was safe after just a few minutes and it was fascinating to be able to have this conversation in real time about how each of us responded. It was the perfect example of each response: fight, flight, and freeze.

The reason for the bear visualization is to show that people who have experienced traumatic events have traumatic responses to visceral reminders of the events. The reason we use the term "visceral reminders" is because they don't always make sense and we often can't make a connection between the situation and past trauma. It would be simple if we could say something like, "this child loses control when someone bumps into her because when she was young she was often hit by her brother". This scenario is possible, but generally things are more complicated than that. For many of these children, there was not only a stressful event (or many repeated events) but also a disruption in development and learning.

When a child (person) experiences a reminder, often called a "trigger", they respond as if there is a threat in front of them at that moment.

The child then goes into fight, flight or freeze mode.

Remember the bear analogy when thinking about this. There is a bear in front of you that could kill you. That is the type of arousal that this person could be feeling. The clue is what is happening in their body. Think about the ways in which you wrote how you would react for clues.

This process is based on neuroscience and has been well researched. If you want to learn more about brain development and the neuroscience of trauma check out the Child Trauma Academy, http://www.childtrauma.org.

As you observe a child who is struggling notice their physical reactions. Is their face red? Are they breathing heavy? Are their fists clenched? If you see these changes occur, the child may be about to fight his way out of the situation.

A simple observation form designed to learn how the child reacts during the progression of anxiety can help parents and educators to understand what is happening for the child. The goal would then be to intervene before the child loses control.

Body Response Observation Form
Student's name _____ Date _____
Observer's name _____
What may have been the stimulus?

Observations during the progression (anxiety)	Intervention Ideas
Facial Expression changes	
Body Language	
Speech	
Mood	
Other	

Sample observations can be found in Appendix 1-J.

People often say that children are resilient and this can be true. The problem is that in childhood, resilience may have meant taking care of themselves for lack of a competent caregiver. Children who have to look inward to solve the trauma that was imposed on them add another layer to the crisis. These children come up with mechanisms to keep themselves safe. These techniques may have even kept the child alive.

When a child like this enters school, these techniques are not needed. There are a lot of adults available who will take care of their needs. They do not have to do it themselves anymore.

These children learned that they can't trust anybody. They most likely have experienced the shame of feeling like they are not worth the caregiver's time or love.

So they enter school feeling like they are not worth anything and they can't trust adults to take care of them. They will use the defense mechanisms that they learned to stay safe. When an adult tells them that their survival skills are not allowed in the classroom, their fear can create internal chaos.

You may have listed some of these above but here are a few more examples of behaviors you may see:

- manipulating or controlling other children
- extremely shy or quick to fight
- running away when a transition is coming
- lying often
- crying over small things
- overreacting when losing games
- trouble staying still or concentrating (hypervigilant to what is going on around her)
- taking things that don't belong to them
- issues with food, hoarding, over eating, hiding food etc.

The two interventions for teachers:

1. Develop a relationship
2. Teach the child how to self-regulate

We will go into more detail about these in the chapter on discipline. When thinking about self-regulation, start by questioning...

What helps you calm down when you are feeling stressed?

_____
_____
_____
_____
_____

Of the methods you listed, what might transfer to the children in your care?

_____
_____
_____
_____
_____

What calms a person down is different for each individual. What is calming for one person can be distracting or even agitating for another.

If you want to learn more about the various types of trauma, check out the National Child Traumatic Stress Network:

http://www.nctsn.org/trauma-types/complex-trauma.

Some answers to the questions from the chapter based on workshop participation:

What and how does a baby learn?

- they learn from watching others
- they learn through their senses: touch, taste, sound, etc.
- repeating motions
- body language
- imitating sounds and motions
- through comfort and distress

What could a parent-child interaction teach the baby?

-trust
-comfort
-self-esteem
-love
-safety
-language

Developmentally what changes when a child moves from infancy to toddlerhood?

- they start to talk
- they become more mobile (walking)
- they become more independent
- they start to pretend
- they ask questions

How does that impact this learning?

- adults have to watch them and keep them safe
- they are constantly testing their limits
- cause and effect thinking (drop things off the table so someone will pick it up)
- pretend play leads to more in-depth copying and repetitive behaviors

What do they learn from caretakers at this stage?

- safety
- limits
- how to recover from mistakes
- what behaviors are negative or positive
- how to ask for help and when to try things on their own
- that they are loved and important
- general right from wrong

What does a child in a dysfunctional situation learn about the world?

- not to trust
- fear
- it's not safe
- it can be painful and uncomfortable
- the world is unpredictable
- that she is unimportant and doesn't matter to anyone

How does it impact the child's developmental learning that we described above?

- They may be afraid to take risks.
- They may not test out or copy language or problem solving.
- Fear causes them to have difficulty socializing.
- They imitate negative behaviors.

What behaviors or emotions might we see in a child with an unhealthy early attachment cycle?

- emotional age is younger than chronological age
- temper tantrums
- angry or sad
- aloof
- disengaged
- difficulty making friends
- self-centered
- clingy
- uncomfortable with negative feedback
- controlling
- dis-regulation
- executive functioning issues
- cause and effect relationships are confusing
- rewards are ineffective
- praise and "good time" have opposite effect
- poor eye contact
- no empathy
- withdrawn

Part II

In this section, the next four chapters alternate between information and suggestions for parents and information and suggestions for educators. The focus of each chapter takes a different perspective. The more we know about every angle the better equipped we are to handle the rigors of education in our society. So whether you are an educator, a parent, or both, you should be able to take away concrete suggestions from every chapter.

TERMS IN PART II

Curious investigation
I use the term curious investigation to mean that an adult focuses on why a particular behavior or event took place by looking for the motivation. It takes practice to be curious instead of frustrated (or at least in addition to frustration).

Child-centered goals are goals set for the child, based on the age of the child and help her to improve from where she started. The child is often included in setting the goals. **Child Centered Consequences** are the same but used when considering discipline.

Available to learn means that the individual is not distracted by physical or psychological factors so they can pay attention to learning. For example, a child who hasn't slept enough may not be completely available to learn.

Strength-based refers to curriculum, goals, or instruction that focus on what the child can or should do rather than what they can't or should not do. A strength-based direction would be to walk rather than, "don't run."

Rudeness: May have different connotations for different people but in this context I am referring to things like a child interrupting an adult, making unkind comments or gestures to others, vocally criticizing or calling people names.

Regulated: A person can become or be regulated. I use the term "regulated adult" when I refer to an adult who is calm and will not change their behavior based on the child's emotions. The adult is able to follow the plans that she made for the given situation.

Attunement is a form of non-verbal communication typically referring to an interchange between a caretaker and a child. The caretaker follows emotional and sensory cues from the child and responds accordingly. The child is tuned into the caretaker's facial expression, body language, tone, timing of speech, etc. It can help the child to learn to regulate.

Activities that promote attunement or help a child practice attunement will be physical yet calming, repetitive, rhythmic, and will often include copying or repeating the actions of another person.

Baseline: A person's relaxed state. Anxiety builds and the person needs to be calmed "down" so they can be at their typical state and available to learn.

Agitated or stressed

Baseline

Sleepy or withdrawn

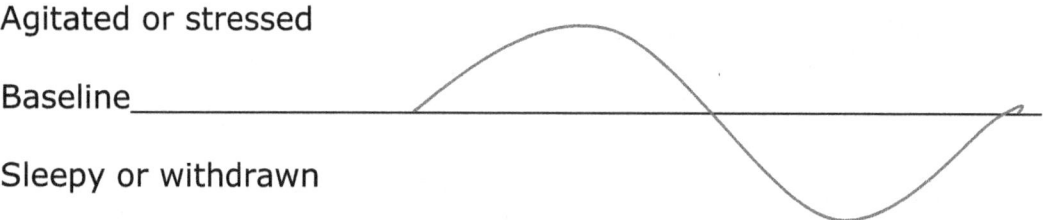

Brain/body activities:
Brain/body activities are exercises or easy body movements which utilize both hemispheres of the brain while making them work in synchronization. Research shows that doing these types of exercises helps students concentrate and engage cognition.

See:
https://www.stylecraze.com/articles/simple-brain-gym-exercies-and-its-benefits/#gref.

Mindfulness, is a mental state achieved by focusing one's awareness on the present moment, while calmly acknowledging and accepting one's feelings, thoughts, and bodily sensations.

*Wikipedia's definition of mindfulness is, "The practice of maintaining a nonjudgmental state of heightened or **complete awareness** of one's thoughts, emotions, or experiences on a moment-to-moment basis".*

This article consists of 20 definitions of mindfulness: https://positivepsychologyprogram.com/what-is-mindfulness-definition/.

Non-threatening body language:
- Never block a student who is having a tantrum or is escalating.
- Keep your body a few feet away from the child.
- Leave your arms down by your side or folded across your chest.
- Do not touch the child who is escalating.

Communicating at the child's level pertains to the child's physical level and developmental level. Sit or kneel so you are face to face with the child. Use developmentally appropriate words in your own voice, not talking down to the child.

Chapter 2
Behavior and Discipline at School

QUESTIONS TO CONSIDER

What has made things harder today than they have ever been before?

Has motivation changed in students? If so why?

Are students more disrespectful than they used to be? If so why?

How can we calm stress and anxiety in the classroom?

A question that I like to ask educators is...

What makes things harder for teachers today than they used to be?

_____
_____
_____
_____
_____

I suggest staff brainstorm this question together. Different things are harder in different communities. In all the times I have asked this question, no one has ever said to me that they don't think things have become harder.

Nationwide we are dealing with:

- poverty – or stress about finances
- increase in suicide
- substance abuse
- drug exposure in utero
- political unrest
- rapid change in technology
- the impact of trauma over numerous generations

What issues stand out in your community?

_____
_____
_____
_____
_____

The reason I start with these questions is because it helps us to consider some of the reasons why we misbehave. Stress leads to negative behavior.

Challenging behavior issues are at the forefront of what teachers do all day, every day. It is what educators always want to talk about in my workshops.

One way to think about behavior is in the same way you think about physical pain. If something hurts in your body, it tells you that something is not right. When a child is behaving in a negative way, she is trying to tell you that something is wrong. Despite how it may seem, children do not misbehave for no reason.

Definition of behavior, according to Webster's Dictionary:

"The way in which an animal or person acts in response to a particular situation or stimulus".

Notice that the definition of behavior indicates that there has to be a stimulus. Behavior doesn't come out of nowhere.

The path to improving behavior begins with curious investigation. This is a hard way to start because negative behavior has an impact on our own feelings. The first thing we think about when a child is acting up does not usually have to do with curiosity.

The most common reason for big negative behavior in people (not just children) is that they do not feel heard. When someone is not feeling like their point is getting across, people tend to raise their voices. Things can then escalate.

Think about a time that someone did not understand you and you became frustrated. How did that make you feel? How did you respond? Before considering an intervention, make sure that the child believes that you have understood what they are saying to you. You don't have to agree with them but they should feel like they have someone who "gets it".

We have to create child-centered goals regarding our expectations around behavior. Think about what your goals are and be clear. You will have goals for specific children, group goals, and community goals.

For example:

1. For the child's self-esteem to improve.
2. For the child to have a calmer, happier, existence.
3. For the child to be available to learn academically.
4. For the class to have more harmony.

The most important goal according to many of my colleagues is to **teach the child social and emotional skills in order to better their lives and their futures.** Interventions should be focused on this goal. Ask yourself, what is the child going to learn from this situation? Or, what does the child need to learn from this intervention? In order for a child to learn from an intervention, the child should be involved with considering solutions. If it is simply a punishment imposed on them, there won't be true social-emotional learning. You may train them to not do the specific behavior again. You may even encourage others to not to try out the behavior. However, most children will find another negative way of getting their message across. Children come away from punishments feeling ashamed and angry. Some children may act remorseful, but the experience will not necessarily apply to other situations in their lives.

You will have an opportunity to make your own list of goals at the end of this chapter.

There are countless reasons why children misbehave so there need to be flexible interventions available.

Three types of behavior concerns that I will address in this chapter are broad issues. The three topics that I hear parents and teachers discussing most are:

- lack of motivation
- disrespect
- moodiness (which can translate into a bad attitude)

Motivation

Why do you think motivation has changed in students?

_____
_____
_____
_____
_____

I have noticed that many students don't seem to care about grades. They don't seem to want adult approval for their work. If something is hard they don't want to do it. They don't seem to appreciate conquering a challenge. This isn't true for all students, of course, but I have seen a massive shift. I studied this for a while and it has changed my approach to some behavior problems around work refusal, as I will explain later in this chapter.

Possible reasons for lack of motivation:

- Traumatic pasts make it so children do not trust adults so they try hard not to care what adults think of them. If they did care, they would be vulnerable to letting adults down which can be painful and damaging to one's self-esteem.

- Larger class sizes make asking for help difficult so they give up.

- Our technology-based society has made it so that we are not used to working with others to overcome obstacles with support.

- Parents may be overworked and not available to children's need for approval, so children are used to not caring about adult approval.

- Students are used to having the technology to fix any problem so they don't think it's necessary to learn things.

What do you see as obstacles to motivation in your setting?

_____
_____
_____
_____
_____

Motivation in young children has to do with relationships.

I often ask people who their greatest teacher was and why they were so memorable. My husband answered the question like this:

"Mr J. was the best. He was really hard but everyone liked him anyway. It isn't even that they liked him, they respected him. You just wanted to do well and behave well because you didn't want to disappoint him".

It takes time to build trust and form relationships with students. Letting students know that you care about them can be a game changer. It has to be genuine. Children need to believe that someone cares if they fail or succeed. This is even more important when students don't have someone at home who is paying attention to their school work.

Rewards

I never believed in rewards for children. I feel that for many children the disappointment of not getting rewards has a stronger negative impact than the positive impact for those that do. Students who are already successful tend to get the rewards and those who struggle don't. Children should learn that the greatest reward is to feel good about their work. I have shifted my thinking in this area slightly because I am concerned about the lack of student motivation. I think we can add some extrinsic rewards in order to begin to build on their work ethic. It takes balance and the understanding that the ultimate goal is to remove the rewards and have the student feel proud of what they accomplish.

When thinking about rewards we want to think about the outcome for those who do not receive them. It should be about success and not about failure. The purpose is to motivate children to try hard, but not shame them into it.

There are two ways to do this.

1. Have the whole class work toward a reward but do not show who has contributed what; each individual will know how much they added to the pot.

2. Come up with individual rewards for students based on their own success rate.

For the whole class, you could come up with many ways to show class progress without naming individuals. For example:

- Every time a student goes up one point from their last grade a marble goes in the jar. When the jar is full there is a class reward (movie, pizza, or extra recess for example).

- When test grades are averaged together and the whole class earns an average of 85% or above, the teacher puts a cut-out square on the wall. When the track of squares gets to all the way around the room, the class gets the reward.

The teacher does the visuals so students do not know who brought the averages up or down but individuals will be motivated to try harder. This also builds a feeling of community.

What are some other ways to do this within your own classroom?

_____
_____
_____
_____
_____

For individual student motivation, try having each student come up with their own visual. They will need to be provided with age-appropriate examples. The students would create their own pictorial chart and color in the chart when they met a goal. The parameters should be set for success. The student could choose their own reward from a list, depending on their interest. It is especially nice when you can bring the larger school community into the incentive.

Some rewards that I have used are:

- lunch with the principal
- lunch in the classroom with two friends
- an extra library book
- time in an older or younger classroom
- time with the physical education teacher playing a sport
- read a piece of work over the intercom
- if a goal has to do with finishing in-class assignments, they might be able to use the extra time to do art or other activities of interests

In the example below, a second-grade student drew a picture of a mountain with a flag on top. His teacher set goals with him.

1. If he finished one of his reading books he could color a square.

2. If he brought in completed math homework he could color a square.

After 10 squares he could choose a friend to play with in the gymnasium for 15 minutes.

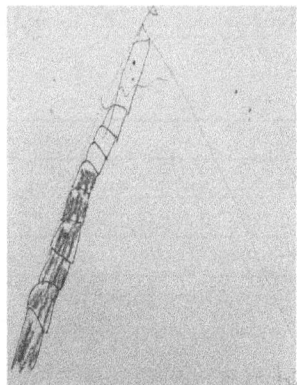

Although everyone is expected to finish their books and do their homework, these things were particularly challenging for this student.

These goals were not public or shaming. The other students didn't know how he was doing unless he wanted to tell them. Setting a goal such as lining up quietly, may have to be judged in front of the other students. These activities should not embarrass the student and should be strength-based.

A third-grade girl drew a path to the sun...

A third-grade boy drew a race car track...

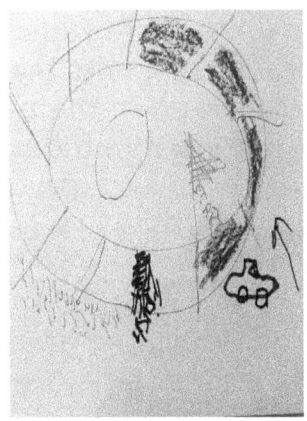

If motivation is an issue for you and you like these ideas, spend some time making lists of your own ideas for whole class rewards and individual rewards. They should motivate without shame.

Respect

Are students more disrespectful than they used to be? How?

_____
_____
_____
_____
_____

What causes children to be disrespectful?

_____
_____
_____
_____
_____

Some children have become extra rude according to people who come from older generations. Adults try to solve this problem using the same methods that worked in the past. Change is hard, but what once worked will not work in today's systems. The list of why things are different today was extensive. Each one of those reasons is also a reason to reconsider how we handle issues with our students.

If a student is rude to an adult, the adult's reaction is often based on how it made him or her feel. Picture a student saying something to you that really pushes your buttons. In one workshop that I ran, for example, a man confessed that when the students were upset they would call him fat. It is disturbing to me that students think that it is okay to say something like that to a teacher! Picture a time that a student said something inappropriate or rude to you.

When a student is rude, what comes to mind before you react?

How dare he talk to me that way?
What gives him the right?

What comes to mind for you?

_____
_____
_____
_____
_____

What actions do educators typically take when a student has been rude to them?

- insist on an apology
- send the student to the principal's office
- keep the student after school

What other methods have you tried in the past and found unsuccessful?

_____
_____
_____
_____
_____

These responses are based on the adult's perspective; therefore, the adult is not necessarily focusing on what their role could be in shaping this child's behavior. They may punish and then move on.

If we took our initial defensive reaction out of the equation and became focused on the child, we might become curious. Why is the child behaving this way? Some people simply think that it is the way that they are being raised, but I encourage you to look deeper. You can change a child's life this way. Children are not born acting a certain way, they are taught. **You as an educator have the power to re-teach them.**

Telling a child that they are being rude does not teach them what rude is or how to not be rude. For so many reasons we have to assume that children do not know how to be kind and socially strong.

Note:

CONSEQUENCES and INTERVENTIONS are two different things.

An **intervention** consists of tools you use to try to teach the behavior. The goal is to have the behavior stop or morph into something that is appropriate. Interventions often take time.

A **consequence** is more like a punishment. Consequences that are done well connect the action to what may naturally occur in the real world. Often an adult doesn't have to impose these on a student but point them out. For example, "I wonder if you did not do well on your test because you stayed up too late last night. What can we do next time to get your grade up?"

Case example:

Jenny was in fourth grade. Her class was not self-contained so she had a different teacher for social studies. Her teacher was male and most students really liked him. One day she seemed to have more energy than usual. She was known as a bit of a troublemaker but today she was especially disruptive. Mr. C. asked her to quiet down and to pay attention multiple times. She kept raising her hand but she was also calling out answers, so he did not call on her for the answer. Upon his third request, Jenny shouted out, "You quiet down dummy". Many students laughed and others sat shocked, waiting to see what would happen next.

Mr. C. took a deep breath and calmly said, "Jenny, I am frustrated and what you just said hurt my feelings. I want to talk to you after class. Now, why don't you go get a drink of water to calm yourself down and then come back and try to stay in your seat."
Mr. C. made it clear to the other students that it is not okay to talk to someone that way. They understand that there will be a conversation and most likely a consequence, but they do not need to know details. He also modeled respectful responses to a difficult situation. His deep breath showed children an appropriate way to calm down during stress. Asking Jenny to take a break and get a drink gave her a chance to reorganize her thinking and it gave her a second chance to try to pull it together.

When we get angry or frustrated we often model the same types of behavior that we are insisting the child should change. Mr. C. made an effort not to do this.

Later, when Mr. C. and Jenny were alone he said, "I am really confused about why you spoke to me like that and called me dumb."

Some children will be able to engage in this conversation at this point, but many will not. In that case, you could offer some possibilities and see if the child can pick one.

Jenny stared down at her shoes so Mr. C. said, "I am wondering if it was because you were mad that I let Crystal go first and you wanted to go first. Or maybe someone in the classroom did or said something you didn't like."

"I am pretty sure it's not because you actually think I am dumb or that you wanted to hurt my feelings. You and I care about each other. That's why I want to figure this out. When people care about each other they help each other correct mistakes, or make amends to feel better about what is going on."

"If you can't tell me what is going on I will just have to assume that it is what I think: you were mad that I let Crystal go first. Did saying those words to me help you get to go first? I am not likely to pick you to go first in the future if we can't work this out. Also, if you say something like that to me again you will have to stay after school so we can have more time to talk about this."

Jenny eventually engaged in the conversation and showed some remorse. This didn't solve all of Jenny's behavior issues, but over time and a few more slip-ups and support, she improved remarkably.

The components of effective interventions in this example are:

- The student was not shamed in front of others.

- The teacher role modeled respectful behaviors.

- The student was shown the natural consequence.

- The student was given another chance to do better.

This exchange taught the child about relationships instead of simply punishing the behavior and taking up more class time.

<u>Moods</u>

In addition to rudeness do some of your students seem moody?

Is this a shift? If so why?

_____
_____
_____
_____
_____

Stress can cause people, including children, to be in a downright bad mood. We are not talking about clinical depression here, just the typical down in the dumps moodiness that many of us notice more and more lately.

Adults have periods when they are in a bad mood but they don't seem to respect the fact that children are the same way.
One thing that I loved about my job as Assistant Principal is that children would often come to me and say "Mrs. P., I have to talk to you".

This statement means a lot. If you have children saying this to you, you have done one of the greatest things that an educator can do. You have earned their trust. This is especially true with children who have had a traumatic past because they do not trust easily. As a teacher in a classroom, it is difficult to stop what you are doing to talk to individual students who request it. We started a system of writing notes. I love this idea because it allows the student to share what they are worried about. They feel like an adult is paying attention. This often helps students stay more focused at school because they know that their issue will be addressed and they stop being distracted by it. Just having it on paper and delivered will often lift a child's mood. I also like to create extra opportunities for children to write. In addition, these notes help the students feel like they are involved in the solution.

For example:

Name: _____ Date: _____ Time: _____
Grade:

Dear Mrs. Porter,

I am angry with:

Because:

You could help me by:

Or...

```
Name: _____ Date: _____ Time: _____
Grade:

Dear Mrs. Porter,

I am angry with:


Because:


You could help me by:
```

Sometimes bad moods and attitude problems come from something serious that is going on in a student's life that we are not privy to. This is why we have to pay attention to moodiness.

Trevor's story

Trevor was a fourth grader with a small build and extra big eyes. He was very quiet and had definitely seen some days that we would rather not know about. He often wanted to talk. I suspected that at times, our talks were to prove that I was there for him, so his topics never seemed very important. It would not usually take up more than a minute of my time so I always listened.

When you earn the trust of students, you have to be extra careful that you don't make assumptions.

One day we were in an assembly when he asked to talk. I asked him to wait until it was over and he sat calmly on the bleacher obligingly. When it was over, he asked if we could go to my office and I suggested we sit on the bleacher because everyone was leaving anyway, that way he wouldn't be as late to class. Again, he obliged without argument.

"Mrs. Porter," he began, leaning in toward my ear, "my dog died yesterday."

I pulled back and looked at his face. His giant eyes were filled with tears. "Oh, Trevor," I stammered. "I am so sorry- let's actually go to my office." I held his hand and he cried silently while we walked down the hall. When we arrived, he sat in the chair across from my desk and I sat in the one right next to him. He had stopped crying and he said,

"So, yah, she was normal until yesterday. I was lying on her bed with her when I noticed that she was breathing funny. Then it seemed like she stopped breathing. I told my dad and then she died. My dad dug a big hole and put her in it. I made her favorite sandwich and put it in the hole and we covered her up with dirt."

Then Trevor stopped to ask me if I was ok and he handed me a tissue.

"And I also wanted to tell you that you might want to check on my older brother (sixth grader) because he said he was taking a shower all night but I could hear that he was crying in there."

"Oh, Trevor, what can I do for you?"

"I guess there really isn't anything unless you know how to bring someone's best friend back from the dead?" His voice caught on this sentence.

I told him that he didn't have to go back to class. He told me he <u>did</u> have to go to class. He said that his parents told him that he would be in trouble if he told anyone about this. They did not want him being sent home from school or crying in school. He didn't want me to tell his teacher or the other children.

So, he went back to class. His brother did not want to talk to me. I checked on them both a lot that day.

These are some thoughts I had after Trevor's day:

- If my best friend died I would not be at school and I would have bereavement support.
- I would not have behaved so poised and grown up if my best friend (or my dog) died.
- I believe that the dog was not only his best friend but one of his only friends.
- If children do not have at least one adult in the building that they **trust**, they will be walking around all day holding onto that kind of pain without any support.
- Teachers typically have no idea what children are going through in their lives when they come into the classroom.

What does this story make you think about when it comes to moods?

_____
_____
_____
_____
_____

I found something called a pocket dog that I gave to Trevor to keep in his pocket. They are small enough so that they won't draw a lot of attention from other kids. I'll admit, I got myself a few as well.

https://www.horsetackco.com/breyer-pocket-box-dogs.html.

Discipline

When I speak to teachers about discipline they often bring up packaged programs. Guidance counselors also run through curriculum that was developed for the masses. Teachers are good at following a curriculum and therefore it is easiest to not reinvent the wheel. Set curriculum also helps schools to keep things consistent.

To prepare children for the real world we should be sure that whatever program we use considers the following:

- Fair and equal are not the same thing. What is important is that children (people) get their needs met and are able to grow from where they are.
- Rewards will not take the place of personal motivation forever.
- School-wide consistency is important but a classroom should also feel like a community within itself.
- Teaching classmates that others are struggling and in need of extra care and support is how we raise compassionate people.

People who understand others and have the ability to listen well tend to be successful. Consider this when setting up rules, consequences, and boundaries for the classroom.

Overall behavior management of a classroom should depend on the population that is in the room. When children start school there should be a basic set of ground rules that can be built upon and tweaked as needed. No one strategy will work for every child in every situation.

Children of all ages should be part of determining what the rules are for their community. When rules get broken teachers should be able to say, "remember we all agreed on this rule".

Interventions

The two interventions listed at the end of the Trauma and Attachment section were:

1. **Build a solid relationship**
2. **Teach self-regulation**

Many components in this book discuss how to build relationships with students such as:

- smile a lot
- be a regulated adult (more about this soon)
- make eye contact
- use children's names often
- get to know their interests
- LISTEN
- be a positive role model
- let them know that you care if they fail or succeed
- write notes

Teaching self-regulation can be challenging.

The first thing is to be regulated yourself. You cannot help a child de-escalate when you are escalated. Your own ability to handle stress is one of the best indicators of positive behavior in the classroom. It is okay to be stressed or anxious but how you handle it is being watched.

Ways to role model stress reduction in the classroom

1. "Ok class, I am getting a little frustrated so I would like us all to stop and take some deep breaths to help me out."
2. "Timmy, this is getting hard, let's both take a stretching break."
3. "I am feeling tense so I would like everyone to do silent reading so I can go to my desk for a calm-down break."

Students need various levels of self-regulation opportunities. Students with trauma backgrounds will likely need you to regulate with them for a while. Some of the examples above could work for that. Your classroom should have the following within the curriculum:

- a way to calm down and re-group where they are (such as at their desk)
- a place in the classroom to go to re-group
- a place or person in the building to go to if they have to leave the classroom

A great way to have students calm down at their desks is to give them laminated cards with breathing activities pictured on them. They can pull them out and practice breathing techniques whenever they feel the need.

Another technique is to have them draw what happened after a stressful incident. You will find a method that uses drawing at the end of this chapter and in Appendix 2-C.

In the classroom, there should be a sensory space where students can go to calm down. The space should be out of sight of the other children in the classroom (if possible). Low light, soft surfaces, stress balls, bean bag chairs so they can sit or curl up are all examples of sensory items that could be included. Items can be added to the space as the year goes on and the teacher learns what tools are effective for certain students. The teacher can provide a sand timer that the child can turn over and when the sand is gone they can try to re-join. This is not a time-out space; the students should be asked if they need a break and never forced to.

These types of self-regulation techniques are given to the students as opportunities to circumvent getting in trouble.

What other items could you picture in a sensory space in your classroom?

_____
_____
_____
_____
_____

What do you do to calm yourself down when you are under stress?

_____
_____
_____
_____
_____

Which of these practices could you model to students? How?

_____
_____
_____
_____
_____

Discuss methods of calming down with your class. Also, discuss ways to help feel better when you are feeling down. Come up with some techniques for the whole class and encourage children to list personal techniques. You can also encourage students to bring this information home and ask them to have a family conversation regarding how their parents reduce stress (when appropriate).

Chapter 4: Educators Building Resiliency will offer more suggestions regarding preventative approaches to behavior and discipline.

List your goals. Keep these goals handy whenever you are thinking about interventions.

What are your child-centered behavior goals for individuals in your classroom?

_____
_____
_____
_____
_____

What are some goals for small groups?

_____
_____
_____
_____
_____

What are some goals for the whole class?

_____
_____
_____
_____
_____

Chapter 3
Behavior and Discipline at Home

QUESTIONS TO CONSIDER

Do your children feel anxious?

Are your discipline strategies working?

How do you handle stress at home?

This book started with an introduction to trauma and attachment, but behavior problems affect all families at one time or another. Negative behavior happens for many reasons. The strategies that we use for trauma-based solutions can be helpful to children and families, even if there is no history of trauma.

Stress

Sometimes adults have a difficult time imagining that their children have stress in their lives, just like we do. It is hard to believe that without bills to pay and a boss breathing down one's neck, etc., life can be stressful. In addition to the anxiety that children often feel, our moods can add to our children's anxiety.

Handling our own stress, our children's stress, and the intersection and impact of each can be challenging. Things get stressful.

The best tool you have to teach your children is yourself. You can be a role model of what to do when things get tense.

There was certainly a great deal of stress when I was a child. I was raised by a single mother of three children who had no child support and no money. My mother worked very hard to get herself out of that situation. She put herself through college and became a teacher. I watched her find resources and support. She sought aid from a church where I learned more about community. I used to have to go with her to her financial aid meetings where I listened to people teaching her how to make it work. She would often do her homework with my brothers and me.

Something has changed about how we interact with our children in the world today. Maybe we are trying to protect them from difficulties, but by doing this, they don't learn how to handle tough situations.

Think about your life with your child(ren). If you do not feel that negative behavior is an issue in your home, you can skip this part.

What behaviors frustrate you the most?

_____
_____
_____
_____
_____

How do you react when you are frustrated by the listed behaviors?

_____
_____
_____
_____
_____

How does your child behave when you react that way?

_____
_____
_____
_____
_____

How do you think your child feels when you react that way?

_____
_____
_____
_____
_____

What do you do to calm yourself when you are frustrated, angry or under stress?

_____
_____
_____
_____
_____

How can you help your child calm down when he is stressed, angry, or frustrated?

_____
_____
_____
_____
_____

How do you handle negative behavior (list from above)?

_____
_____
_____
_____
_____

Make a list of techniques that you have tried at home that have been successful (however you choose to define "success").

_____
_____
_____
_____
_____

Make a list of strategies you have used at home that have NOT worked well.

_____
_____
_____
_____
_____

Do you notice any patterns? Are there similarities between your child's feelings and your feelings?

_____
_____
_____
_____
_____

Think of negative behavior as your child making a mistake. We learn from our mistakes and so negative behavior can be a teaching tool. You are your child's first teacher. You are the teacher who knows your child the best. You are the teacher who spends the most amount of time with your child and has witnessed all stages of development.

Preventative strategies:

- Be clear about rules, boundaries, and consequences.
- Set clear limits that are straightforward and simple.
- Whenever possible, let your child know what the consequences of breaking rules will be.
- Be prepared for them to make mistakes, and be prepared to follow through.

You will find examples at the end of this chapter.

Intervening with negative behavior:

I call this method D.E.A.R..

D.E.A.R. stands for :
De-escalate
Explain
Amends
Reconnect

De-escalate

If possible, do not start working out a behavior issue with your child unless you are BOTH completely calm and level-headed. The chapter on resiliency will offer strategies to de-escalate and become focused on the problem.

Explain

Keep it very simple and direct:

1. This is what you did wrong.
2. This is why it was wrong.
3. This is what you should have or could have done.
4. This is the consequence of the behavior.

Many people leave out the teaching part of this. Teach your child how to do it right in the future, do not overly focus on the mistake. If and when appropriate, turn the third statement into a question such as, "What could you have done instead of what you did?" Explain the impact of the behavior on the child's life. If you spelled out clear consequences ahead of time it should be a matter of simply stating what the imposed consequence is. If there are natural consequences, you could ask the child what is going to happen now that she behaved in that way. In some cases, there may be both natural and imposed consequences.

Amends

Help your child find a way to fix his mistake.

Reconnect

For your child to learn conflict resolution skills and to maintain a close family bond, always reconnect after an incident. Find a clear way to let them know that you love them even when they make mistakes.

Here is an example of what D.E.A.R. could look like:

De-escalate

Mom:
I am so frustrated that you hit your sister that I need to take a few minutes to cool off. You sit down over there and calm yourself down too, and then we'll talk.

(Mother models stretching and breathing to calm down.)

Explain

Mom: You hit your sister even though you know that in this family we treat each other with respect. What should you have done instead?

Child: Use my words.

Mom: That is right. Sometimes you have to take a break and calm yourself down so that you are ready to use your words when you are extra mad.

Mom: Why did you hit your sister?

Child: Because she took my markers.

Mom: Did it help? What is she doing now and what are you doing now?

Child: She is drawing and I am talking to you.

Mom: If you hadn't hit her, she might be the one in trouble for taking your markers.

Amends

Mom: I want you to write her an apology note like we talked about.

Reconnect

When she brings her mother the note they read it together and make any changes needed. The mother says something positive about the note.

Mom: I like how you wrote the note with a green pen and wrote neatly.

In this case, I might also facilitate a discussion between the two children.

These types of lessons take time but they stay with children when they leave the house. Like Jiminy Cricket, your child needs to learn to have a conscience. After a few of these lessons, the child in the example may be at school feeling like she wants to hit someone when she hears you speaking in her mind saying, "Calm down and then use your words". Your lessons eventually turn into their own values. Teaching values takes time; it isn't done after one incident.

I have a podcast where parents can call in and ask behavior-related questions. I will give you a few examples from various age groups.

Case Example:

Alex

Alex is a three-year-old who has tantrums at school and at home. They are worse when he is tired but he also has trouble sleeping. His teacher reports that children are starting to choose not to play with him because he gets so upset when he doesn't get his way. Tantrums at home are infrequent but they happen when his parents say "no" to something that he really wants. They have tried time outs, ignoring him when he has a tantrum, and offering rewards if he makes it a week without a tantrum.

Some reasons why children have tantrums:

- people are not listening to them
- they are having trouble communicating what they want to say
- they feel like they do not have any control over the situation
- there are often changes to what they are expecting to happen
- they feel like they are rushed
- there is too much stress and anxiety in their lives

Suggestions:

A counselor or play therapist might be helpful in this situation.

Find out what precipitates the tantrums at school. What does "doesn't get his way," mean? Is he always with the same children or does he do it with anyone? How have teachers handled it?

Notice what is happening when he tantrums at home. One example from this child was that he didn't want to stop playing and get ready to go.

Give him a warning before a transition. "Alex, in 10 minutes we are going to put the puzzle away and get ready to go to grandma's." Another warning at five minutes. A sand timer is good for this, too. He can flip it himself and that will help him feel like he has some control over the timeline.

If getting ready to go is stressful, give yourself more time and continue with warnings. Break it down: "You need to have your coat on before the sand is gone"; "Put your shoes on before I count to ten." Have consistent routines for transitions. Give the same warnings every time in the same order until he does it himself.

Notice how he is behaving right before the tantrum starts. Name it for him. "Alex, you are starting to get frustrated. Let's take a few deep breaths and then make a plan together."

Do not get escalated with him. Stay calm and speak softly. Sometimes children will stop a tantrum because they want to hear what you are saying: "Alex, you are very upset and I would like to help you calm down". If possible, walk away until he calms down. In the same soft tone say, "I am going to walk away for a minute, when you are calm I am going to help you."

Make eye contact and show that you are hearing him when he is protesting. "Alex, I know that you want to keep playing and you are upset that we have to leave. Let's try to think of ways that you could feel better. Could we put your puzzle in a special spot for when we get back tonight?"

If transitions are part of the problem, transitional objects can help - especially if he has some control over it. Every time that you go to grandma's, have him draw a picture to take to her, for example. Or have him be in charge of bringing her the newspaper.

Try not to change your answer or give in when he has a tantrum. If you have to change your mind, explain your reasoning when he is calm.

Address the Sleep Issues:

- If you are comfortable, try dietary supplements (check with your pediatrician first).

- Talk to your pediatrician about the sleep issues.

- Make sure bedtime is the same every night.

- Have a consistent bedtime routine.

- Don't allow electronics or overly active play for an hour before bedtime.

- Make sure he is hydrated and not hungry when he goes to sleep, but try not to have him eat an hour before bedtime.

- Talk to other parents about what has worked for their children.

Michelle

Michelle is 6 and loves to ride her bike around in the driveway. Her parents are trying to teach her to take care of her things and have asked her repeatedly to put the bike away. Her father was so frustrated that he told her that he was going to give her bike to the scrap metal garage and she would never see it again. Mom thought it was harsh but wasn't sure what they should do. They tried taking the bike away, but the very next time she left it out again.

I thought about the D.E.A.R. approach in this situation:

De-escalate: "I am sorry that I said I would hurt your bike but I get frustrated when I ask you something over and over, and I feel like you don't listen. I will not do that to your bike but let's talk about it and make a plan."

Explain: "When you leave your bike out it is in the way of the car. If we hit it with the car, it would break your bike and hurt the car. Someone could also take it, and we know that it is special to you. What should we do to help you remember to bring it in? From now on every time we find it out, we will put it away for two days."

Even though this had been tried once, I feel like it needs to happen consistently for a few times before it will sink in.

Amends: I had a hard time thinking of a way Michelle could make amends to her parents for not listening; but when we came to this part Michelle's father came up with the idea of doing yard work together around the driveway. He told Michelle that he needed some help and that this would be a way for her to show him that she was sorry.

Reconnect: The yard work also worked for them to reconnect. When dad brought out some bulbs to plant that Michelle would see whenever she rode her bike past them, the connection continued.

Brenda

According to her mother, Brenda is a well-behaved nine-year-old. Lately, however, she has been rude to her mother and acts a bit moody for no reason. I asked her mother to do a little investigating and get back to me.

- Is she eating, sleeping, and hydrating?
- Is there additional stress in her life?
- Is she hanging around with different friends or has she lost friendships?

These are all important questions when you are assessing the behavior of a school-aged child.

When mom got back to me a week later, she had found the answers to these questions but also worked some of them out by the time we talked. Brenda is getting more sleep, eating better, and hydrating. Her stress level is about normal. She does have a new friend from school that she has been talking about.

I asked mom to invite the friend over and observe the girls together and then call me again.

When she called she was incredulous and sounded a little embarrassed. "Why didn't I think of that? It was very obvious when they are together. She is behaving just like her new friend. It's obnoxious. Do I tell her not to be friends with that girl?"

Suggestions:

- Get to know your child's friends as best as you can.
- Reward healthy relationships and be clear about why.

When she finds friends who seem to be good role models, reward those relationships. Invite them over. When your child asks why that friend and not another, tell them the truth. "I like how polite he is and he is easy to have around."

I don't recommend forbidding friendships. Be honest without insulting the friend or the friend's family. Discuss friendships with your child without necessarily bringing up certain friends.

Ask questions such as:

- What do you think makes a good friend?
- How would someone who is not a good friend behave?
- What would you do if a good friend wanted to do something you didn't like?

Talk about the importance of being an individual and how a good friend's personality could complement each other rather than being identical.

Go through the names of classmates and have her tell you what is good about each person and ask if she has ever been friends with that person, why or why not?

Try not to use the term "don't like", but point out behaviors without adding judgment:

- Amy talks extra loud when she wants something.
- Amy's voice didn't sound understanding when she told you not to do that.
- Gretchen always says hello to me when you bring her into the house.
- Gretchen seems to really like you, she compliments you a lot.

All of this effort will help in the long run. You and your children will get into a rhythm of talking about the friends she hangs out with. If you are not overly judgmental, she will confide in you. She will share the good things and the bad and possibly start to agree with you. Eventually, this will help when she starts to date. We need to be comfortable talking about the pros and cons of our children's romantic interests.

My daughters each dated one person that I did not approve of, one when she was 18 and the other when she was 22. My first daughter ended up telling me that she wished she had listened to me. The second daughter often said to me bluntly, "I wish you liked Tony." I had to be honest and say, "I wish I did, too."

My last bit of advice for this chapter is to take good care of yourself. Find balance in your life. Take a class, join a support group, start a book club, find online support.

What could you do to add balance to your life?

_____
_____
_____
_____
_____
_____

How could you manage your time so that you can do what you listed?

_____
_____
_____
_____
_____

Chapter 4
Educators Promoting Resiliency

QUESTIONS TO CONSIDER

How can you set up an environment that promotes resilience?

What do you do when a student is having a hard time?

How can you support a student with a traumatic past while working with the whole class?

When I was asked to create a follow-up to my trauma presentation, I did some investigating regarding what topics would be most helpful for educators. The majority of teachers and providers were looking for advice on de-escalation techniques, and ways to build resiliency education into the curriculum. Much of this chapter is based on the presentation that I created.

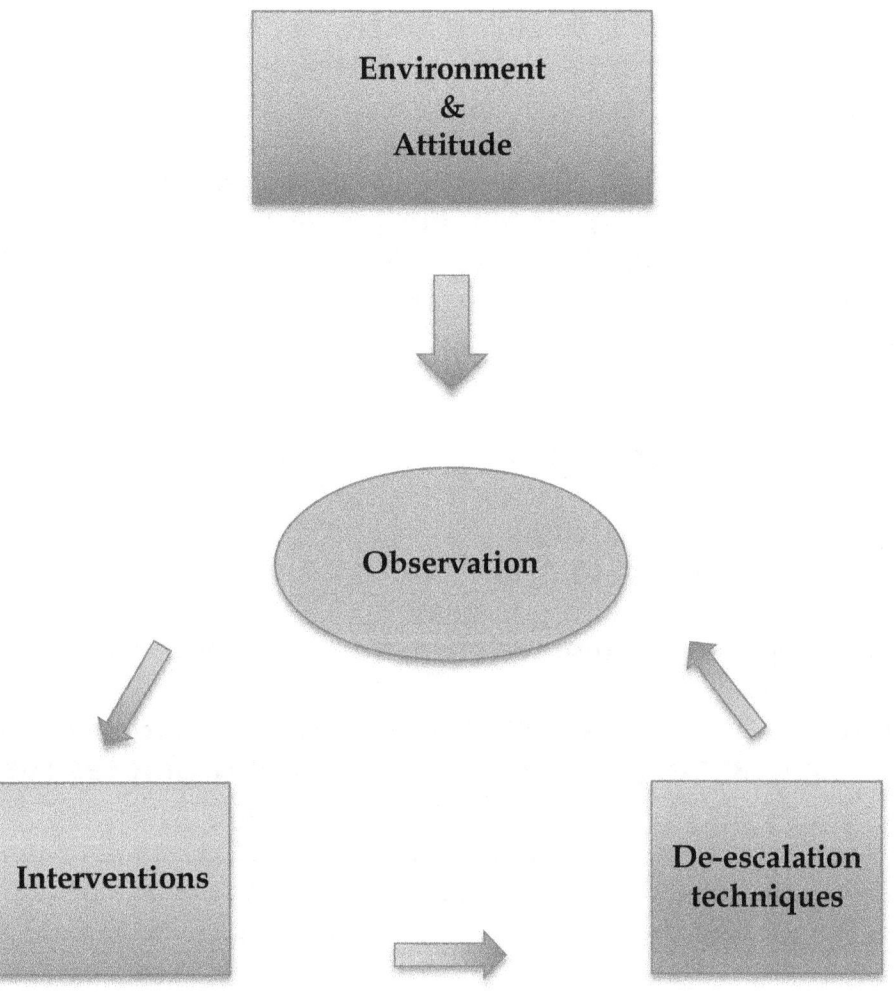

When working to advance a child's capacity for resilience, it makes sense for us to focus on prevention as well as the outcomes which often manifest as tantrums (fight, flight, freeze behavior). Our goal should be to teach children better coping mechanisms to navigate the world. We also want to help students improve their self-image and promote trust in others.

Start with empathy. Even if you believe that the child is in the "wrong", you can still respect their reality. Begin from where the child is. Believe that the child's experiences have a direct impact on his/her behaviors.

Three areas I suggest teachers focus on are the environment, attitude, and activities. Based on what we learned from the first section of this book, "Overview of Trauma and Attachment", think about these three areas within your classroom.

ENVIRONMENTS

Think about environments that are conducive to:

- action to calm activities
- books that relate to a variety of experiences and cultures
- calm, cozy places to get away
- the opportunity to move away from a trigger (not locked in)

Thinking about what you learned about trauma, how else might you arrange an environment that promotes resiliency?

_____
_____
_____
_____
_____

Once again, empathy is important for setting up environments with individual child's needs in mind.

ATTITUDE

- be with children with the understanding that they are trying their best
- use non-threatening body language
- communicate on the child's level
- use a soft tone of voice
- smile
- use humor
- LISTEN before you react or respond
- role model:
  - ➢ desired behaviors
  - ➢ conversation that promotes relationships
  - ➢ your own stress reduction/de-escalation

What else might you do to improve outlook?

_____
_____
_____
_____
_____

ACTIVITIES

What are some activities for the age group you work with that help practice attunement and build trust between you and your students and between the students themselves? These activities should involve the brain, body, repetition, patterns, and reciprocity of actions. They should not be competitive activities. How do you think the following activities build attunement and trust?

- drumming
- yoga
- swimming
- horseback riding

What are some other activities that would improve resiliency by building the capacity to trust?

_____
_____
_____
_____
_____

Teachers should become trauma informed. This will lead to a more in-depth understanding of development, trauma, attachment, and the over-all need for stress reduction.

Educators should be comfortable Investigating and reassessing, this leads to personal, on-target interventions.

Now put the intervention pieces together:

Trigger

Examples of triggers for a particular child:

- Can the trigger be eliminated?

- Do there seem to be many or few?

- Are there triggers that can be anticipated (such as transitions)?

- What are your clues that the child has found an obstacle?

Escalation

- What can you do to intervene early in the progression of the anxiety?

- How do you know that the intervention is working?

Results

- What does baseline look like for this child?

- Over time with particular interventions does the child return to baseline more quickly?

- Have you helped the child reconnect and repair the relationship?

DE-ESCALATION TECHNIQUES

- The first and most important thing to understand about de-escalation is that it is more about YOU than about the child.
- Do not expect the behavior (or the feelings) to disappear in an instant.
- Do not set strong limits while de-escalating.
- Talk as little as possible (more talking will = less listening).
- Do not raise the bar or let the child feel trapped (power and control are not the goals).
- Think about secondary triggers.
- Be a role model (and not for negative behavior).

Remember your empathy:

Put yourself in the child's place. Understand or accept what they are going through to the best of your ability.

DE-ESCALATION GOALS IN ORDER OF IMPORTANCE

1. Safety: What do I have to do immediately so people are safe?
2. Calm: What can I do to help this child feel calmer?
3. Solutions: What can we do so that it won't get to this point the next time?

DE-ESCALATION STATEMENTS

- I am listening to what you are saying.
- I understand that you are frustrated.
- I am going to keep us both safe while I learn what is frustrating you so much.
- I am going to hold that for you until you are calm and ready to have it back.

Notice that these statements begin with "I" and not "you". "You" statements while a child is escalated is about blame instead of results. The time to explain what the child did wrong is not when they need to be de-escalated. "You" statements can cause the child to feel shame and then to escalate further.

Other de-escalation statements:
_____
_____
_____
_____
_____

Teaching regulation strategies:

- The best way to learn what will work with a particular child is to watch and listen and do not make assumptions. Do not assume you know what the child is feeling, thinking, or needing from you before you watch and listen.

- If the child is anxious and has outbursts or temper tantrums, ask someone to observe and look for trigger, escalation, and result. What would have helped this child before she got to the end result? When we are in the middle of the situation we cannot see the subtleties that children experience. There is always a reason for behavior. The reason is not usually one that comes from an immediate adult frame of understanding.

- Come up with interventions, give them time, and then have someone observe again, and then tweak the interventions. Changes in interventions are almost always necessary because growth means change and progress which means as the child changes, so do their needs.

- Learn what reduces anxiety and calms this particular person.

Intervening at the "teachable moment"

Many tantrums and outbursts happen because the child feels "backed into a corner" or stuck. Try to intervene with enough flexibility for them to get out of their own messy situation.

Use open ended questions and statements versus closed ended

- "What are we going to do?" versus "You have to", or "You better".
- "This seems extra important to you", versus "You shouldn't feel that way", or "you are overreacting".

Interventions should...

- Be individualized to fit the child's needs and situation.

- Be appropriate for the developmental age of the student.

- Help build trust.

- Teach about appropriate behavior.

- Teach about effective social interactions; reinforce the value and benefit of connection with others.

- Reinforce the concept of cause and effect thinking.

- Not cause shame.

- Reinforce the idea that the world is a safe, predictable place.

What else is important for you to consider within your own classroom?

_____
_____
_____
_____
_____

Mindfulness

I have been adding some workshops on behavioral interventions through mindfulness to my platform. The topic of mindfulness could be a whole other book (in fact the topic will have a bigger presence in my next book).

Teachers who practice mindfulness report that it has a big impact on their outlook. They are able to be good role models and know how to teach it to children. There are many books available that will suggest mindfulness activities for the classroom (see "Resources" at the end of this book). My favorite idea is to have a deck of cards and pull out a random activity each day. Read it to the class and do it with them so it is a surprise to you, too. There are many types that you can order or you can make your own. I like…

Mindful Games Activity Cards: 55 Fun Ways to Share Mindfulness with Kids and Teens Cards – by **Susan Kaiser Greenland** (Author), **Annaka Harris** (Contributor).

On the following page there is an outline for trauma-informed strategies for the classroom that I developed for a third grade class. We added timing for each piece so that the teacher could see that it wouldn't take up too much of their instruction time.

Morning meeting: 10 minutes

Create a comfortable space in the room where kids can gather; sitting on the floor would be best. Morning meeting should be ritualistic, the same components in the same order each morning.

For example...

1. Everyone in the room greets each other in a new way every day. Pick from a jar but each one should require eye contact and a phrase and should be modeled first (ex., today walk up to each person and wave your elbow at them and say good morning).

2. Two Important Questions:

   ➢ Raise your hand if you had a good night sleep.
   ➢ Raise your hand if you had a healthy breakfast.

   This may motivate them to do better and it also gives the teacher information.

3. Around the circle:

   Everyone lists one thing that they want to do super well today (give examples when first starting).

4. Teacher gives the whole class one goal for the day.

   Example: "Today's goal is for the whole class to **walk** in the hallway on the way to specials". Or, "Today's goal is for me to hear extra kindness in the classroom."

5. Stretching exercises.

During Class

Brain/body activity <u>for every 15 minutes of sitting still</u>, 2 minutes

Movement - Team building <u>every 45 minutes of sitting still</u>, 5 minutes.

Movement activities should be deliberate and include calming down at the end.

Movement is a good way to combine rewards and feeling good about work completion. It also adds team building, taking a work-break, and exercise. An example is the silent koosh ball game (described at the end of this chapter). A movement break is good to do when most of the class finishes an in-class assignment.

It is important that we not hold kids back from doing these activities even if they don't finish the work. We also shouldn't deny the whole class if one or two kids doesn't finish. This is for community building.

Laughing breaks – <u>after work completion break</u>, 5 minutes.

Show a video clip of people laughing. This usually causes contagious laughing.

End of the day meeting – quick process …What went well, what will we do better tomorrow. 10 minutes.

Incorporate some classroom jobs specific to certain kids so they have a stronger sense of belonging, based on their strengths. Ex: JB, something broke can he try to fix it? TB, the math manipulatives need to be sorted and make a color-coded list of what we have.

This is a method we adapted from the book Comic Strip Conversations, by Carol Gray. Also suggested by Joelle Van Lent in a workshop, Vermont 2018.

To have children process their feelings, therapists draw stick figures and have the children tell them what to write in the word bubbles. We turned it into a worksheet where the children can write or draw themselves.

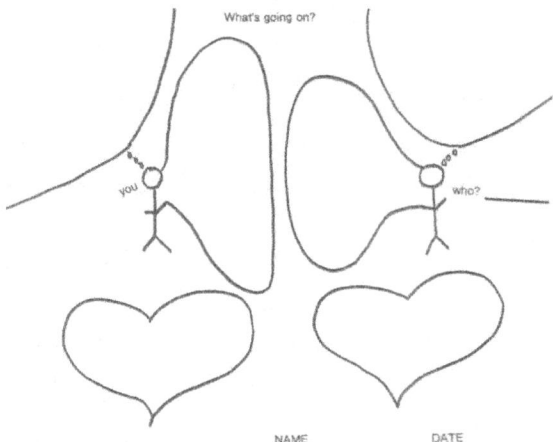

The bubble that is attached to the hands and the head represents what the child said or did. She writes or draws about what happened. Then she is asked to try to take the perspective of the other person and write or draw what the other person said or did. The thought bubble above represents what she was thinking and what she thinks the other person was thinking. The heart represents what she was feeling and what she thinks the other person was feeling.

Then she tells the adult about the picture.
Next, she draws what she could have done differently.

I am often surprised at how well children do with perspective taking.

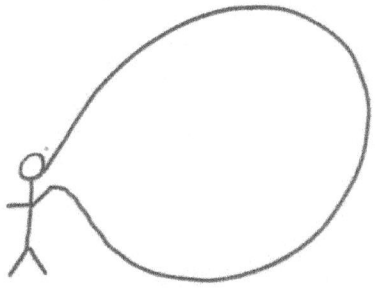

What could you have said or done differently?

In the example below, the second grade student wanted to put the solution on the same page as the problem. He included both children in the solution picture instead of filling out the one with just himself. I noticed that he had a target on his body which led to an interesting and important conversation.

This is another example of a solution picture. She thought they should both say they were sorry and think kindly about each other.

This example is from a third grade boy who was sent to the principal's office. His whole body was electrically angry. According to his explanation of the drawing, the teacher was happy because she was evil and liked to make him suffer. Notice that what the teacher was thinking was that he should be sitting in his chair, which was accurate.

The teacher in this situation needed to reconnect with the student and I am not sure she would have realized the importance of that without this illustration.

QT Ball

This is a game that my friend Diane Bailey uses in her fourth or fifth grade classrooms. QT stands for quiet teamwork.

Line the students up in two lines facing each other across the room. No one is allowed to talk during the game. The students toss a large koosh ball to the person across from them and this continues down the line. The teacher keeps track of how many catches they get as a team. They try to beat their last record.

It is important to discuss how it is not just the catcher that drops the ball, the thrower and the rest of the team's support influences if the ball is a catch or not. The students all cheer without sound. Be sure the class is supportive when someone drops the ball. Ask them how they might show support without words.

I noticed students making silent clapping gestures toward each other, patting each other's backs when a ball fell, and a lot of soundless excitement and energy. Something about the silence causes them to calm down faster after the game.

Chapter 5
How Parents Strengthen Resilience

QUESTIONS TO CONSIDER

What is hard about school for your child today?

What has changed since you were in school?

How do you feel that your child's school rates compared to your own experiences?

What is different?

Is it common for your child(ren) to give up easily or act like they don't care about their work? Why do you think this is?

What makes school different today from when you were young?

- The stress we are under may be affecting our children.
- Technology.
- Class sizes.
- The number of standardized tests.

What else is different?

_____
_____
_____
_____
_____

Parents often talk about how the "difficult" children in the classroom who make it harder for their child to learn. Some teachers feel the same way. It is the *troubled* children that are to blame for the teacher's distractions and inability to teach to the whole class.

This isn't untrue.

I hope that in the future people will continue to work together. I worry that everyone will live on their separate computers and human interaction will no longer be necessary.

In my opinion, for our best possible future, parents will teach their children how to work and live in a community. Children need to learn to work well in small groups or teams, not only in isolation.

Every child has something unique to offer. The problem is that people tend to focus on each other's weaknesses. Teachers are charged with improving children's learning so they have to start by noticing what they are not good at. What we need to do is to set obtainable goals to make progress.

Don't deny what is difficult for your child - recognize it and motivate them to do better. Then look at their strengths and realize that these traits are the ones that will most likely, if nurtured and encouraged, help your child find success throughout life.

What did you like and what were you good at when you were a child?

_____
_____
_____
_____
_____

Any connection to the things that make you happy now?

_____
_____
_____
_____
_____

The best thing you can give your child is the compassion and intellect to understand others. That, in combination with their passion, will make them a leader. To lead you need to understand other people's challenges and their strengths and how you can put them together to accomplish big things.

Your child has to know that true success can't be achieved in isolation, it has to be done by understanding how she needs support and finding just the person who can fit into that part of the puzzle.

Some of the students in the classroom who are taking up all the attention and who are not always kind to your child are going to be the best teachers they will ever have.

There are two major complaints that I hear from parents about the "other children" in the classroom:

1. "Other children are distracting, making it hard for my child to learn."
2. "Other children can be unkind or aggressive."

Distractions

If your child complains that a student's behavior is distracting, instead of becoming upset with the distracting child, the teacher, or the school administration, think about this: the most educated people know how to learn despite distractions. Instead of role-modeling more complaining or frustration, help them practice creating solutions. Help them build techniques that will strengthen their ability to learn. Have this discussion with your child even if they have not complained about other students' behaviors. Make a list together. See what ideas your child can come up with on their own.

Some suggestions that parents and children have shared with me:

- Ask the teacher for a different place to sit.
- Politely let the other student know that the actions are bothering you.
- Tell the teacher that you are feeling distracted by the behavior and ask for suggestions.
- See if you can do your work while completely ignoring the distraction.

Can you think of other suggestions that you may give your child?

_____
_____
_____
_____
_____

Unkind or aggressive behavior

Even if your child feels like another child can be aggressive you can help him feel more in control of the situation. You can encourage your child to have conversations with the appropriate people and then you can follow up.

- If your child witnessed another child being aggressive tell him to report this behavior to the teacher and the guidance counselor (or other appropriate adults) every time it happens. Not just the teacher.

- Talk about the difference between tattling and helping to keep your community safe.

- Have your child find an adult in the building that they trust. They can build a relationship with this person and then be able to discuss their concerns with someone outside of the classroom. An assistant principal, a guidance counselor, a specials teacher or a teacher from a past year can all be good candidates.

- Teach your child advanced social language such as, "I am going to leave this area because I have seen you hit people and I don't want to be near you unless I am sure you won't do that." Or have them tell the teacher that the child is making them "uncomfortable."

- Even though it is sometimes tempting, teaching your child to retaliate is not helpful. You do not want to encourage her to be a victim, but you want her to show adults that what is happening is not a two-way street. Help her to eliminate all the "he said, she said" possibilities.

Follow through

- Keep the conversation between you and your child comfortable so that they want to share issues with you.

- Write down what your child reports to you and the dates. If you hear of a similar issue a second time, call the teacher. If it happens a third time call the principal.

- If there is an incident after a report to the principal ask for a meeting with the teacher, the guidance counselor and the principal (see the chapter on advocating for your child at school for more information).

- Be aware that when you report issues to administration, by law, they cannot tell you what consequences are given to the other child.

Note: The recommendations listed are not intended for a situation where your child sustained an injury from another child. If there is an injury, call a meeting that includes the nurse and the principal then send a description of your entire experience to the superintendent.

List other ideas that you and your child come up with for dealing with unkind classmates:

_____
_____
_____
_____
_____

One of the best gifts you can give your child is to have a stable relationship with his teacher. The two of you should give the impression that you are a team. Don't speak negatively about the teacher in front of your child. Encourage your child to discuss issues directly with the teacher, and then you can call and ask the teacher how the conversation went.

Similar to what I suggested for your child, you should try to build a relationship with someone at school, in addition to your child's teacher. If your child is having an issue at school, having another staff member who can go into the classroom and observe can help.

Understand that the information that you receive from your child is almost always only part of the story. Not necessarily because your child isn't truthful, but because they won't always notice or remember nuances.

CASE EXAMPLE:

Kate has two children. Haley is in 5th grade, and Paul is in 3rd grade. Kate describes Paul as a rough and tumble kind of kid. When the school called her, she assumed Paul was misbehaving again. When she heard that Haley had been in a fight at school, she thought there must have been a mistake. The principal explained in a rushed authoritarian voice that Haley was with the nurse because she had some sand thrown into her eye.

Kate's first reaction was rage. She wanted the phone number of the other child's parents. She wanted that child expelled. She knows that Haley is a sweet, kind, quiet child who has never been in trouble in school.

Kate and I talked on her way to the school. Below is a list of some of the things I suggested (even though none of this was easy for Kate):

- First of all, do some breathing exercises and calm down. Try to put your anger on hold until you hear the whole story.

- Kate does not like or trust the principal. Because of this, I had encouraged her to build a relationship with the guidance counselor, so the two of them talk often (although usually about Paul). I told her to ask the guidance counselor to be present when she spoke to the principal.

- Even though she was angry, I suggested that she try to start with an open mind because that is what is best for Haley. I asked her to listen to the whole story and try not to feel like she had to defend Haley (yet).

- Next, look to Haley tell the story, with the understanding that it might not be the complete picture. Try to listen without interruption. Ask open-ended questions and assure her that you are on her side and you are there to help her.

This is what the principal said:

"The children were outside when the teacher heard yelling. She approached and saw Haley pushing another student. The teacher sent Haley to the principal's office. She was crying. Her eyes were red from crying, so they didn't notice right away that she had sand in her eye and it was swelling. When they noticed it, she went to the nurse." The principal interviewed the other children and then called Haley in.

According to his findings, Haley had insulted the other child and poked her in the arm. The other child pushed Haley, who fell into the sand. When she stood up, she yelled and pushed the other child, and that is when the teacher came upon the girls.

Kate told the principal that she wanted to have a conversation with her child with the guidance counselor before he discussed consequences. She stayed calm and asked Haley what happened. Haley told her mother that she tapped the girl on the shoulder and said to her that her hair was stuck (it was caught in her earing). The girl turned around and yelled, "Your hair is sick." Haley's friend tried to help and rushed in too quickly and bumped Haley into the other girl. The girl pushed Haley hard, and she fell into the sand face first. She was so embarrassed that she got up and yelled, "What the hell is your problem," and pushed the girl back. Everyone started yelling, and that is when the teacher came over.

Some form of these events is pretty typical at school. The other child probably had a traumatic background and being tapped from behind triggered her fight response. Unfortunately, what often happens is that the parents get angry because their child was hurt and is punished. They react with anger at the school. Principals are often automatically on the defensive about this because they deal with angry parents often. The children have consequences without the adults fully understanding the whole story.

The girls needed the opportunity to realize the misunderstanding and work through it without the parents and administrator's personal feelings getting in the way. School personnel are not often skilled in this type of mediation. They can be busy and defensive when dealing with parents.

The most important thing in these situations is what your child learns from the encounter. Point out the things she did right and ask her how she might have done things differently.

If it were my daughter, I would have told her that I didn't blame her for getting up off the ground and reacting after she was treated that way.

It is interesting because I have counseled many parents to teach their children NOT to use violence. Parents often say to me, "I don't tell them to hurt anyone...unless someone else starts it. I teach them to defend themselves."

It is not that simple, though. There are many variances in every human interaction.

The fact that Haley never had problems fighting with others yet took such a bold stance when other methods were not working shows that she has a solid foundation of empathy and confidence (self-love).

Kate took a firm stance with the school. She wrote down Haley's accounts of the incident which the guidance counselor had also heard. She suggested in writing that the girls have the opportunity to talk the situation through with support from the guidance counselor or another adult that all parties trusted. She hoped that the girls would have some input into what would happen next.

She wrote that she appreciated the teacher's and administrator's diligence in this situation but that she would not accept any consequences without a meeting that included the superintendent. She cc'd the guidance counselor, the other girl's mother, (small town, she was able to figure it out), and the superintendent. She let Haley read the letter before she sent it.

Kate is a very busy person, but the time she took to meet with the principal, talk to her daughter at the school, and write the letter, was well worth it. She was able to teach her daughter about handling a difficult situation and keep her relationship with the school intact. At the same time, she gave the school the message that she will not take these types of issues lightly.

In the end, with Kate's patience and understanding, this event turned into a learning experience for Haley. It could have quickly turned into a situation that was traumatizing for her and in which the other child was labeled a bully. Haley understood that there are people in the world that did not have a mother like hers and a happy upbringing and that in the future she will have knowledge regarding how to help, or walk away from issues.

Chapter 6
Characteristics of Your Own Resiliency

One of the best teaching methods I know:
The word, "oops".

Are you resilient?
This is an important question for educators and parents.

What does resilience mean to you?

_____
_____
_____
_____
_____

In what ways are you resilient?

_____
_____
_____
_____
_____

What makes resilience difficult for you?

_____
_____
_____
_____
_____

YOUR ROLE

Do we put obstacles in our own way? We are ALWAYS role models for children. We model the good, the bad, and the ugly. Children watch us make mistakes. The good thing is that they also see us react to mistakes, make amends, correct ourselves, etc.

One of the best educational phrases can be "oops". You can show children that you make mistakes too, and show them how you handle it.

Tips for building resilience

- Treat stress as a challenge to overcome.

- See problems as mistakes and learning opportunities.

- Focus on the truth of a situation and on what can be done – try not to overthink it or dwell on it so that it becomes bigger than it is.

- Notice how you respond after a crisis. Think about what you would change about your response if you could.

- Utilize and build on your social supports.

- Participate in your community or create community through book clubs, parenting groups, or classes.

- Be positive; don't let negative thoughts take over.

- Exercise every day.

- Do something peaceful every day.

- Focus on what went well at the end of each day.

- Keep a journal of accomplishments and successes.

- Practice self-appreciation. Learn to feel good about yourself.

- Develop and track realistic goals. Again a journal is great for this.

I took a year-long training to be a life coach. We learned a lot about life during that time. I was trained by Martha Beck and I highly recommend her book, Steering By Starlight. I also recommend Byron Katie's book, Loving What Is.

At one of the workshops a woman explained how she sets personal goals. She makes a poster every month and puts it on the refrigerator so the whole family can see it. Her goals are things like:

- Walk in nature for 20 minutes.
- Spend 10 minutes being quiet or meditating.
- Write for ½ hour daily.
- Get together with friends once a week.
- Eat healthy.

She put stars next to the goals that she accomplished each day. She wrote her reward at the bottom of the poster.

20 stars = A Sunday afternoon beach day, alone or with a girlfriend.

She put the chart on the refrigerator to teach her daughters about setting and accomplishing goals and finding balance. She found that her husband and children became very supportive of her goals and helped her to achieve them. Her daughter would notice if she didn't have her walk and bring her hiking boots to her.

I do a chart in my journal where I color boxes when I accomplish a goal. I love when I get a page full of color.

When I was going through a period where I felt extra anxious I kept a worry journal. I wrote down everything that I was stressed or worried about, then I would go back and write how things turned out. After a few months it was clear that I did a lot of worrying for no reason. Big worries ended up being worked out with simple solutions. I also noticed patterns between lack of sleep, lack of exercise, and other physiological reasons why my anxiety was high.

Think about how the following affects your relationships

Defensiveness:

_____
_____
_____
_____
_____

Confidence:

_____
_____
_____
_____
_____

Defensiveness and confidence are polar opposites in my mind. The key is to increase confidence without ego.

How can you improve through mindfulness?

_____
_____
_____
_____
_____

If you want more information about how to think about your own traumatic past go to the SAMHSA website and read about the ACEs studies. ACE stands for adverse childhood experiences.

SAMHSA - Substance Abuse and Mental Health Services Administration

112

Chapter 7
How to Advocate for Your Child at School

The story in the chapter on parents promoting resiliency offers an example of how to work with schools when discipline issues arrive. It has also been suggested to form a good relationship with your child's teacher. You can also teach your child to build their relationship with the teacher at the same time.

- Plan short meetings or discussions with the teacher when things are going well.
- Encourage your child to learn about their teacher's hobbies, family, etc.
- Be sure to have your child greet his teacher every day. Make eye contact and ask how he or she is doing. Also pointedly say goodbye and have a good evening.
- Ask your child questions about how the teacher's day was.
- Send in notes often letting the teacher know things like when your child is extra tired because he didn't sleep well, or when there is stress at home that might affect his day.
- Celebrate events, holidays, birthdays, etc. by making something with your child for the teacher.

The time spent on this relationship will help your child learn to respect people in leadership roles and how to get along with others in general. It will make things easier when issues arise because there will be a level of trust in each other. Having the skills to build these relationships will help your child in work situations for her whole life.

I wrote the following outline for a workshop for a foster care and adoption conference. I did a presentation with my friend Janet Benoit Connor from the University of Vermont Training Partnership. It was called, How to Advocate for Your Child at School. It was meant mostly for students with special needs but the tips can be good for any parents.

ADVOCACY STEPS

1. Start with education: educate yourself.

Make a list of the people who are on your team with their contact information.
Include the best communication tool they prefer to have you use, such as e-mail, school phone, home, etc. This team will differ if the child is on an Individual Education Plan (IEP) or a 504 plan.

- teacher
- guidance counselor
- social worker
- school nurse
- special education director
- additional advocate
- principal
- others?

It is important to build a positive relationship with these folks when possible, **before** issues arise.

2. Educate the school.

Decide if it is necessary to call a meeting...
- before school begins
- after the first few weeks of school
- *or* if writing a letter with a follow-up phone call to the interested parties could suffice

If there is an IEP (Individual Education Plan) or a 504 plan, there should be a meeting held, but in some cases it is helpful to have it scheduled before school starts.

Consider what kind of information you will share with the school.

- What is required that you share?
- What would be helpful to share?
- What types of things might you share at another point in time?
- What should you consider not sharing?

If needed, ask for an educational support team (EST) and have a meeting (if there is no IEP or 504 and a letter and phone calls are not enough).

During meetings try to have an advocate with you that is hearing the same information as you are. Sometimes when we are nervous or frustrated we hear things differently or miss parts. Your advocate can discuss the meeting points with you afterward. This person could be part of the school team or it could be a family member or a support person from outside the school. It should be someone whom you trust and feel comfortable with; ask for copies of the meeting notes.

As part of the meeting or initial contact, create a communication plan for *when there is an issue at school or at home.* This plan should include information regarding:

- What issues or behaviors merit a call from school?
- What is the best way to reach you?
- What is the follow-up plan going to be at home?

3. Issues may arise during the school year.

- When a child is disciplined at school be sure to check to see if the lines of communication are working the way that you previously agreed to in your plan. If not, remind the teacher and others who were involved how you would **prefer** to be notified. Do this **in writing** so that there is a record of the conversation; it is helpful to talk to them in person or on the phone as well.
- When something comes up at home that should be shared with the school, be sure the communication is working in the best interest of the child. Talk to the teacher about the best method for follow-up with you. In this situation, verbal communication with a follow-up e-mail can also be helpful. *It is always a good idea to have a written backup of conversations*.
- Re-configure the communication plan if needed.
- If it is still not working call a meeting.

Communication plans often have to be revised throughout the year after they have been tested. It is helpful if you go into the process with that understanding and to use that language with the school.

4. More proactive ideas and resources:

- Suggest that the school receive training on topics that have impacted your child, such as grief and loss, adoption, race and culture.
- Suggest that the school connect with local organizations that pertain to your child's life.
- Suggest that school staff read this book.

Chapter 8
Educators Mediating Issues with Parents at School

De-escalation
The way into positive relationships and the way out of stress.

Empathy

There are two parts to empathizing with a frustrated person:

> 1. Empathize regarding the current struggle, even if you feel defensive.
>
>   Realize that the feelings involved with a parent regarding their child
>   are intense. Picture a mama bear protecting her cub.
>
> 2. Think about the fact that this person could have some other significant stressors in their life.

I consider myself a kind person. I love to make people laugh, and I like to pull strangers out of a bad mood. I also think of myself as a skilled mediator.

However, there have been many instances where I have been dealing with a particular organization or issue, when I became the person that I never wanted to be. One such situation stuck with me. I became angry with a person representing an organization who made a mistake and took it, in my opinion, way too lightly. The person on the phone was short and was not answering my questions or explaining what had happened.

We often had parents calling or coming into the school very angry about what I would consider small issues. I became good at de-escalation with these families.

My experience with the frustrating phone call helped with this. I thought about what drove my anger that day. It was fear. I panicked, not only about what was happening, but what could have happened. Later I was able to feel grateful that those things didn't happen, but at the moment I wanted someone to help me and not mistreat me. I realized that people in those positions work with angry people like me all the time. They are burnt out and defensive. They don't make the rules but are expected to explain them.

When I got off the phone that day I wrote down the conversation and then I wrote down what she could have said that would have been helpful. It was a useful exercise that led me to consider my own reactions as well as how to help people who are frustrated.

The following information coincides with all of the de-escalation information for children in this book, but I would like to offer some concise advice when dealing with angry parents. It was always hard for me but these methods made a difference.

These are the tips I created when I turned the conversation around:

1- **Empathy** – without admission of wrongdoing.

> "Wow, let me help try to figure out why that happened."

2- **Make yourself human.**

> "I hope you are having a good day – aside from all this, of course."

If there continues to be anger, it often helps the person understand if you say ...

> "I know you are not angry with me; I am only here to try to help you, but I am starting to feel uncomfortable because of your tone. I want to help you figure this out."

3- **State the Facts without judgment.**

   "Ok, from looking up the record, this is what I can see."

4- **Explain the options.**

   "Here are some suggestions and this is who you can call to provide more feedback regarding the concerns you shared with me."

A father came into school unannounced one day and demanded to speak with me. He was furious because his daughter told him that another child had slapped her in science the day before.

I was tempted to say, "That can't be true, how could that happen with the science teacher in the room. I would have heard about it…"

Instead, I used my new tools.

1- **Empathy** – without admission of wrongdoing.

   "Wow, no wonder you came right in today. That is upsetting."

2- **Make yourself human.**

   "Have a seat and let's figure this out. I understand that you are angry, but I am going to do what I can to help. I hope we can talk this through without you continuing to yell at me because it is making me uncomfortable."

   The father's face flushed. It seemed that he didn't realize that he
   was yelling.

3- **State the facts without judgment.**

   "I am going to have to get to the bottom of this. Do you want me to pull your child out of class and deal with it right now, or do you want me to handle it at recess and then we can talk again?"

Asking for his input helped the father feel a little more in control of at least part of the solution. I was glad that he told me that he would be okay waiting. I promised to call him later in the day.

4- **Explain the situation and the options.**

When I called him I said, "This is what I learned. I spoke to your daughter and the other young lady who was involved. I talked to them separately and then interviewed another student in the class. Then I spoke to the teacher. This is the story I got from all of them:

Your daughter and her friend were fooling around, and her friend meant to pretend to slap her but caught part of her cheek by mistake. Your daughter said that it didn't hurt, but some of the other kids were laughing and so she got mad at her friend. The teacher did speak to the girls after class and thought that it was all worked out. There was not any kind of mark on her cheek. Today I got the girls together, and they talked it through some more. I spoke to the whole class and the teacher about roughhousing during class."

I told him to talk to his daughter that night and that we could talk more if he thought further action was needed.

I often said this to parents to help them feel involved. I would not add consequences for a child based on what one of the parents wanted, but I could still listen to their thoughts on the subject. I would explain that I could not tell them about consequences for other children, but would reassure them that I listened to their concerns.

If that wasn't enough for the parents, I told them that they could put their concerns in writing to the principal and if they wanted to they could include the superintendent. This method worked for us because otherwise, the parent would start from the beginning with the principal. They very seldom took this next step, but when they did, I would send in my accounts of the situation in writing as well.

Proactive Tips

- Most schools send home a student handbook with rules and regulations. The rules and regulations should be sent home another time on their own. Consequences of actions should be spelled out clearly. Parents and the student should sign that they have read and understood them.

- Build relationships with parents. Have family events. Make times when you are available to chat with parents.

- When there are consequences, it helps if you have the child write down what happened in their own words so that you can share it with the parents.

Meet with as a staff and come up with more proactive tips for working with parents:

_____
_____
_____
_____

Conclusion

I believe that it is important when learning about trauma and resilience as well as behavior management that the format be interactive. It also must be action-based. There is a lot of abstract theory that is fascinating. The research about the impact of trauma on neurology is comprehensive and valuable. We need to also focus on how it impacts each of our lives and how we can make improvements within our culture.

Educators and parents are in the position to make a difference. With more thinking and more talking and collaborating, we can change the world. You are the most important people in our society with the most impact on our future.

Let's raise good people!

Acknowledgments

I have been to many presentations on attachment, trauma and resilience. I have also presented at conferences with very talented partners. This book was written from my thoughts, experiences, and opinions. Any similarity to book content or presentation content is coincidental.

I would like to acknowledge people and presenters who shaped my knowledge over the years.

I have attended presentations by these authors and professionals: (see bibliography page for more information)

Dan Hughes
Bruce Perry
Bessel van der Kolk M.D.
Kevin Creeden, M.A., Director of Assessment and Research at the Whitney Academy in East Freetown, MA.
Martha Straus, PhD. Professor of Clinical Psychology, Antioch
David Melnick, NFI Vermont
Joelle Van Lent, PSY. D. Vermont

My partners in Vermont, although already mentioned, deserve extra acknowledgement:

Karen Crowley, Easter Seals, Vermont Adoption Consortium, Agency of Human Services
Nancy Birge, Casey Family Services
Janet Benoit Connor

Cover art by Jesse Azarian

First round editors and over-all support, Burt Porter and Janet Porter – THANK YOU!

I want to thank my husband Erik Porter for his patience, advice, support, and love. He has been there every step of the way.

Resources
Suggested Reading:

Bruce D. Perry, M.D., Ph.D. –

Born for Love: Why Empathy is Essential – and Endangered (coauthored with Maia Szalavitz)

The Boy Who Was Raised as a Dog: And Other Stories from a Child Psychiatrist's Notebook

What Traumatized Children Can Teach Us About Loss, Love, and Healing (coauthored with Maia Szalavitz)

Brief: Reflections on Childhood, Trauma and Society

Laura van Dernoot Lipsky –
Trauma Stewardship: An Everyday Guide to Caring for Self While Caring for Others (coauthored with Connie Burk)

Judith Herman, M.D. –
Trauma and Recovery – The Aftermath of Violence – From Domestic Abuse to Political Terror

David Emerson and Elizabeth Hopper, PhD –
Overcoming Trauma through Yoga – Reclaiming Your Body

Dana Caspersen –
Changing the Conversation: The 17 Principles of Conflict Resolution

Bessel van der Kolk M.D. –

The Body Keeps the Score: Brain, Mind, and Body in the Healing of Trauma

Susan Kaiser Greenland and Annaka Harris –
Mindful Games Activity Cards: 55 Fun Ways to Share mindfulness with Kids and Teens

Suggested Reading for Parents:

Daniel A. Hughes –
Building the Bonds of Attachment: Awakening Love in Deeply Traumatized Children

Matthew Sockolov –
Practicing Mindfulness: 75 Essential Meditations to Reduce Stress, Improve Mental Health, and Find Peace in the Everyday

Suggested Websites and other digital media:

The National Childhood Traumatic Stress Network:
 https://www.nctsn.org/what-is-child-trauma

Trauma Center At Justice Resource Institute:
 http://www.traumacenter.org/

Trauma Stewardship:
http://traumastewardship.com/

Still Face Experiment video
 https://www.youtube.com/watch?v=apzXGEbZht0

Appendix of Activities

1– Workgroups, staff meetings, and discussions

- Behavior Discussion
- Assumptions/Bias Form
- Fear and Resilience Form
- Strength-Based Statements Form
- Trigger, Escalation and Results
- Escalation and De-escalation
- Relationship Builder
- Role Model Calming Activity
- Body Response Observation
- Body Response Observation examples 1 and 2.

2– Activities for children

- The Six Whats
- Name Those Movements
- What's Going On?
- Solutions
- I Need a Break
- What is Respect?
- Respect
- Notes to Adults

1– A
BEHAVIOR DISCUSSION FORM

Group discussion –

Answer the following questions with the whole staff. Brainstorm each one on chart paper then place them in a line on the wall. Discuss differences, positive and negative reactions, etc.

What student behaviors frustrate you the most?

How do you react when you are frustrated by the listed behaviors?

How do the children behave when you react that way?

How do children feel when you react that way?

What do you do to regulate yourself?

How can you help your students regulate?

**1-B
ASSUMPTIONS/ BIAS FORM**

What are your own trigger points?

Circle the following items that "get under your skin":

loud noises	the silent treatment	tattling
crying	high pitched sounds	whining
yelling	hitting	name calling

Others:

_____
_____
_____
_____
_____

Now circle the ones that your student(s) seems to resort to when escalated:

loud noises	the silent treatment	tattling
crying	high pitched sounds	whining
yelling	hitting	name calling

Others:

_____
_____
_____
_____

Do you notice similarities or patterns?

If so, what does that mean to you?

1-C
FEAR AND RESILIENCE FORM

What are 10 things that your students may be afraid of?

1.
2.
3.
4.
5.
6.
7.
8.
9.
10.

What are they worried about?

1.
2.
3.
4.
5.

What factors make them resilient?

1.
2.
3.
4.
5.

1– D
STRENGTH-BASED STATEMENTS

Write each statement in a strength-based/resilience-focused format:

She is ruining it for the rest of the class.	
He always lies.	
She is mean.	
He likes to push my buttons.	
She can't sit still for more than 5 minutes.	
He is so disruptive.	

1-E
TRIGGER, ESCALATION, AND RESULTS

Child # _____

Trigger
What are some examples of triggers for this child?

Can these triggers be eliminated?

Are there triggers that can be anticipated?

What are your clues that the child has found an obstacle to dealing with the trigger?

Escalation
What can you do to intervene early in the progression of the anxiety?

How do you know that the intervention is working?

Results
What does baseline look like for this child?

Over time with particular interventions does the child return to baseline more quickly?

Have you helped the child reconnect and repair the relationship?

1 – F
ESCALATION AND DE-ESCALATION

What are some of this child's triggers?

Can they be eliminated?

Which ones can be anticipated?

Signs of escalation or de-escalation: Strategies:

1.
2.
3.
4.
5.

IS OVER THE TOP:

1.
2.
3.
4.
5.

WHAT DE-ESCALATION TECHNIQUES HAVE/COULD HELP HERE, OR WHAT STRATEGIES WOULD HELP REFOCUS THE CHILD?
(a child that is withdrawing instead of having a tantrum).

1 – G
RELATIONSHIP BUILDER

Make a list of ways that a teacher can build a relationship with a child.
Share with each group to make one master list; put check marks next to repeated items.

1.
2.
3.
4.
5.
6.
7.
8.

List students with whom you would like to have a stronger relationship and why.

What techniques from above might you try?

Report back next meeting.

1 – H
ROLE MODEL CALMING ACTIVITY

List methods you can use to role model calming down.
Share with your group:

1.
2.
3.
4.
5.
6.
7.
8.

List methods you can use to calm the whole class.

1.
2.
3.
4.

Write down your favorite answers from other teachers in your group.

What methods will you try this week?

Report back.

1-I BODY RESPONSE OBSERVATION

Body Response Observation Form
Student's name _____ Date _____
Observer's name _____

What may have been the stimulus? _____

Observations during the progression (anxiety)	Thoughts/questions
Facial Expression changes	
Body Language	
Speech	
Mood	
Other	
Intervention Ideas:	

1-J EXAMPLE

Body Response Observation Form

Student's name ___J.P.___ Date _____
Observer's name ___Teacher___

What may have been the stimulus? _Another student took his pen._

Observations during the progression (anxiety)	Thoughts/questions
Facial Expression changes Wide eyes Clenched lips Face slightly red	Is he trying to restrain himself?
Body Language Hugged his body Stomped his foot	Signals next level of frustration
Speech Voice lowered	Again - restraint?
Mood He seems to have a shorter fuse when he comes in grumpy	Why is his day starting
Other	

Intervention Ideas:
— Talk to parents about morning routines — hungry? tired?
— Teach him how to calm body when frustrated — check in w/ an adult

have parent fill out one of these.

1-J, 2 EXAMPLE

EXAMPLE PARENT FORM

Body Response Observation Form
Student's name: JP
Observer's name: Mother
Date: _____

What may have been the stimulus? N.A.

Observations during the progression (anxiety)

Facial Expression changes
He tends to get red and looks frustrated

Body Language
He looks like he might hit someone but then he runs away. Sometimes kicks something.

Speech
Can get loud or soft

Mood
Worse when tired

Other

Intervention Ideas:

Thoughts/questions
What are other students doing to frustrate him?

Activities for Students

2-A
THE SIX WHATS

Name: _____ Date: _____

Write or draw...

What am I great at?

What am I good at?

What subject am I the best at?

What subjects am I good at?

What subjects might I need to work hardest at?

What subject am I going to need extra help with?

2-B
NAME THOSE MOVEMENTS

NAME THOSE MOVEMENTS

With your students come up with a list of as many movement activities that can be done in the classroom and make a list.

Such as:

- situps
- push-ups
- jumping jacks
- hopping
- stretching to the ceiling
- toe touches
- etc.

Assign a letter to each activity starting with A and go through the alphabet.

A= Sit-ups
B= Push-ups
C= Jumping jacks
Etc.

Have the students spell out their name by doing the physical activities.

Try spelling other words all together as a class.

Once in a while announce that everyone should do "Q" or "Z"

2-C
WHAT'S GOING ON

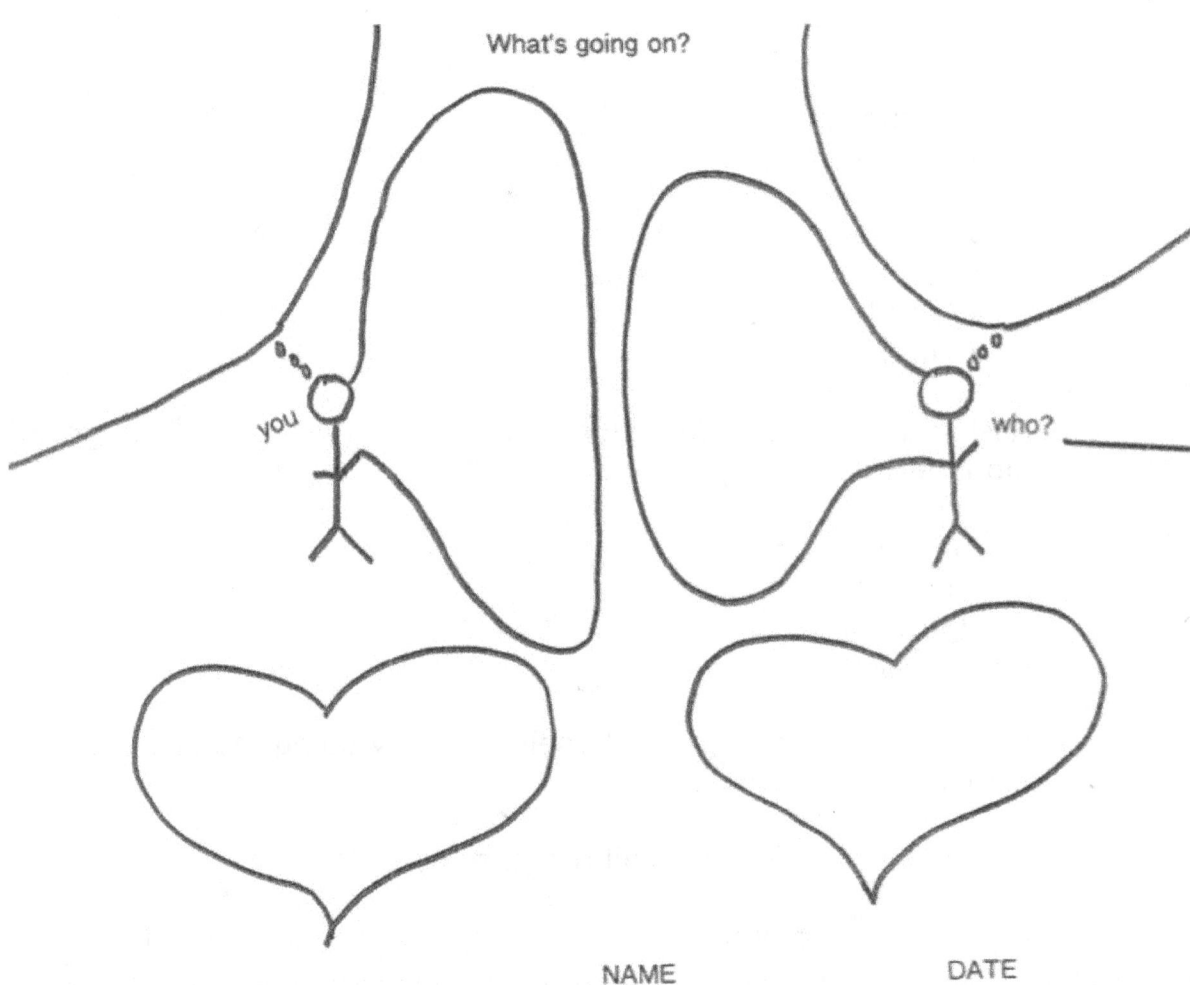

NAME　　　　　　　DATE

2-D SOLUTIONS

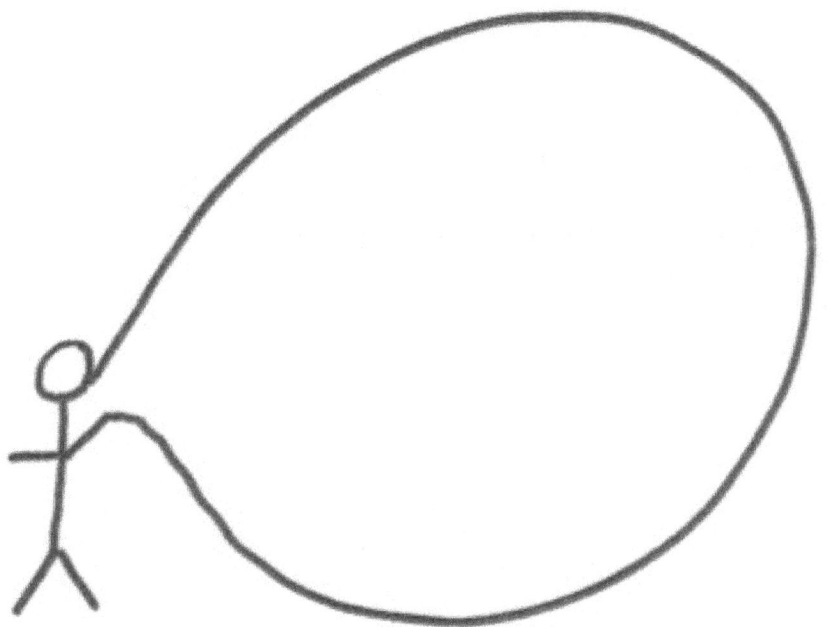

What could you have said or done differently?

2-E
I NEED A BREAK

Name: _____ Date: _____ Time: _____

Right now

Sometime soon

I want to talk to:

I want to speak with the guidance counselor

I want to sit alone for 3 minutes

I want a short walk (2 ½ minutes)

2-F
WHAT IS RESPECT?

NAME_____DATE_____

WRITE THE WORD "RESPECTFUL" OR THE WORD "DISRESPECTFUL" NEXT TO EACH WORD OR PHRASE.

I DON'T WANT TO_____

I DON'T UNDERSTAND THIS PART_____

CAN YOU HELP ME WITH THIS? _____

I CAN'T_____

LEAVE ME ALONE_____

I FEEL LIKE I NEED A SHORT BREAK_____

I'M GOING TO GET A DRINK_____

MAY I GO AND GET A DRINK? _____

I HATE YOU_____

I'M FRUSTRATED_____

What are some of the ways you show disrespect with your tone of voice?

What are some of the ways that you show disrespect with your body language?

What are some ways that you show respect with your body language?

What are some of the ways that you show respect with your tone of voice?

**2-G
RESPECT**

Ask your teacher if you want help with this part.

These are the respectful phrases that I am going to use this week:

1.
2.
3.
4.
5.

Respectful ways I am going to behave:

1.
2.
3.

Disrespectful behaviors that I am going to change:

1.
2.
3.

2-H
NOTES TO ADULTS

Name: _____ Date: _____
Time: _____ Grade:

Dear Mr(s). _____,

I am angry with:

Because:

I think you should:

Name: _____ Date: _____
Time: _____ Grade:

Dear Mr(s). _____,

I heard or saw something that you should know about:

I think you should:

www.ingramcontent.com/pod-product-compliance
Lightning Source LLC
Chambersburg PA
CBHW080513110426
42742CB00017B/3094